THE POLITICAL
ECONOMY
OF THE
NEW LEFT

THE POLITICAL ECONOMY OF THE NEW LEFT

AN OUTSIDER'S VIEW

SECOND EDITION

ASSAR LINDBECK

Institute for International Economic Studies
University of Stockholm

Foreword by PAUL A. SAMUELSON
Massachusetts Institute of Technology

New York • New York University Press • 1977

330.973
L74 p2

m R

Copyright © 1977 by Assar Lindbeck
Library of Congress Catalog Card Number: 77-83267
ISBN: 0-8147-4979-8

Library of Congress Cataloging in Publication Data
Lindbeck, Assar
    The political economy of the New Left.

    Includes index.
    1. Economics—History—United States. 2. Radicalism
—United States   I. Title.
HB119.A2L55   1977   330'.0973   77-83267
ISBN 0-8147-4979-8

CONTENTS

PREFACE

THIS NEW edition of my short book *The Political Economy of the New Left* includes, in addition to the original text and the foreword by Paul Samuelson, some samples of the discussion generated by the book. Thus a short anthology of recent discussions of New Left economists has in fact been included as "Part Four" in the book. The contributions comprise discussion papers by George L. Bach, Stanford University; Robert L. Heilbroner, New School for Social Research; Bruce McFarlane, The Australian National University; Frank Roosevelt and the late Stephen Hymer at the New School for Social Research; Paul Sweezy, writing in *The Monthly Review;* and James Tobin, Yale University. I have also included a rejoinder to some of the criticism, as well as a paper that attempts to see the economics of the New Left in the context of economic-systems analysis.

ASSAR LINDBECK

PREFACE TO THE FIRST EDITION

MY PURPOSE in this short book is to try to interpret, understand, and scrutinize the economic ideas of the New Left. In particular, I shall attempt to discuss, in order, some of the more important questions on political economy taken up by this movement, *inter alia* to facilitate a dialogue between the New Left and academic economists. I shall emphasize some of the main social and economic problems raised by the New Left, rather than give a detailed account of "who said what." This means, in fact, that the book is an attempt to make a contribution to the field of "comparative economic systems." It should be emphasized that the "systematic" distinctions and classifications are mine rather than those of New Left literature.

The book was written against the background of my experience of political debates and the political literature circulated at various U.S. campuses during 1968–1969. The exposition is based on addresses to the Graduate Economics Students' Association at the Massachusetts Institute of Technology, Cambridge, Massachusetts; Columbia University, New York City; and the University of California, Berkeley, all given during the spring and summer of 1969. Somewhat shorter editions in Swedish and Danish were published in 1970.

I am grateful to William Baumol, Peter Bohm, Alf Carling, Frederick Clairmonte, and Stefan de Vylder for their comments on an earlier version of the book.

ASSAR LINDBECK

Institute for International Economic Studies,
University of Stockholm
April, 1971

FOREWORD

THE NEW LEFT is an important movement in the history of ideas. It is an important ideology in the political struggle for men's minds. It is the continuation of an important strand in the development of economics and the related social sciences, and represents a growing discontent on the part of students with what they are being taught in the universities.

Yet where can the open-minded reader go for a detailed discussion and evaluation of the basic tenets of the New Left? There of course are no shortages of tracts and treatises written by radical critics of the social order. And, if all you want are vituperative denunciations of any ideas newer than those of Herbert Spencer or Friedrich Hayek, there are plenty of books and Rotary speeches glorifying free enterprise and condemning atheistic communism. But no one, before Professor Lindbeck, has had the patience to collect together the various notions of the New Left, sift and analyze them, and finally to give an unsparing evaluation —involving both critique and acceptance—of their validity and limitations.

THE STRANGER AS JUDGE AND JURY

Thirty years ago, when the Carnegie Foundation sought to commission an objective study of America's racial problems, it turned to a Swedish economist, Gunnar Myrdal. Precisely because Myrdal came from a society that lacked our racial heterogeneity, he would be able, it was hoped, to arrive more nearly to objective truth. And so it turned out: *An American Dilemma* by Myrdal is not only one of the few classics in the social sciences, but, in addition, it alerted us and the world to the fact that we were an unconscionably divided house, only superficially in a state of equilibrium. The fundamental decisions by the Supreme Court, the Civil Rights movement, the struggle toward integration—all of these things which have become commonplaces were foreseen in the Myrdal study.

Once before it was from the pen of an outsider that America came to know itself. Precisely because de Tocqueville was a Frenchman, rather sympathetic to much in the ancien régime that had vanished with the French Revolution and rather unsympathetic with the nascent notions of American individualism, he was able to discern and extrapolate the characteristic features of a new society. If I wish my face to be drawn as it is, I must not go to my lover. Nor to my enemy. Only what is seen for the first time can be perceived in its uniqueness.

But not any stranger can pen the likeness of a revolutionary movement. Political economy must be grateful that Assar Lindbeck happened to be a visiting professor at Columbia University in the academic year 1968–1969. The right man was at the right place at the right time. To economists, Professor Lindbeck needs no introduction. Appointed at a comparatively early age to the prestigious chair in international economics at Stockholm University, Dr. Lindbeck is one of the young turks in Swedish economics. His grandsires, so to speak, were the great Swedish economists of the First World War period, Gustav Cassel and, above all, the incomparable Knut Wicksell. (Wicksell, who wrote one of his books from jail, never hesitated to speak out in good causes however unpopular: his views against marriage, against the monarchy, against religion, and against a Swedish standing army on the Russian borders kept him from a university post until the age of almost 50; his view that the worker would gain more in real wages from a non-Marxist evolution of the Welfare State lost him popularity in other circles, a fact which inhibited him from speaking his mind not at all.) Lindbeck's immediate teachers were of that vintage generation of Swedish economists: Myrdal, Bertil Ohlin, Bent Hansen, Erik Lindahl, Erik Lundberg, Ingvar Svennilson—but really the list is too long to enumerate.

Assar Lindbeck, though, is his own man. As a schoolboy he saw with his own eyes the flirtations with Hitler's super-race doctrines to which some Swedes succumbed in the days of the successful *blitzkrieg.* No ancient doctrine of Swedish neutrality has kept this soldier in the army of humanity from criticizing, criticizing bitterly, the United States policies in Vietnam. Just as in this country most economists have been associated with the critics of the ruling elite, the business elite—favoring the Democratic programs of the New Deal, Fair Deal, New Frontier, and Great Society, rather than the rugged individualism of Herbert Hoover and/or Barry Goldwater or the moderated versions of Eisenhower and Nixon—it has always been my impression when visiting Sweden that most of the economists there have been rather critical of their own Labor government. Economists, apparently, tend to be perverse! Lindbeck, however, is one of the economists who has been a defender of the general policy of the Social Democrats, though a "friendly (sympathetic) critic" of many details. It is germane to mention this because, if you are too far away from a social movement, you rarely have the interest or the competence to appraise it. Every day of his life, a Social Democrat is fighting through in his own mind the great issues of egalitarianism and efficiency with which the New Left is now engaged. No wonder then that when he visited Cambridge, New York, and Berkeley, Professor

Lindbeck kept his ears open to hear what was being said; and kept his mind open to evaluate the sounds heard. Moreover, a scholar trained in the European tradition can, thank heaven, be expected to know a good deal about the writings of Fourier and Owen, Proudhon and Kropotkin, Marx and Engels, Luxemburg and Lenin, Sorel and Gramsci, along with the more recent writings of Baran, Sweezy, Mandel, Mills, Cohn-Bendit, and Galbraith. Hanging up a picture of Che in your dormitory room is only the first step on the way to understanding the laws of motion of capitalistic development.

THE TEXT BEFORE US

During his sojourn in the United States, Professor Lindbeck was able to try out his first drafts of this book on audiences in Cambridge, New York, and Berkeley. It says something for the complacency of American economics that, prior to Lindbeck's lecture at MIT, many of our graduate students had thought of the New Left as having something to do with politics, not with honest-to-goodness economics.

The Swedish version of this book was published in paperback form under the title, *Den nya vansterns politiska ekonomi*. So resonant was the response, that the book was soon translated into Danish; and a Finnish translation is now in the works. This present expanded American version is not a translation from the Swedish, but an English text prepared by Professor Lindbeck.

Who ought to read this book? I fear that those who need it most are least likely to crack its pages. Those who believe that Milton Friedman's modernization of Adam Smith is all one can know or needs to know about economic policy will hardly be tempted to spend an afternoon studying Lindbeck's evaluations of notions about manipulated consumer preferences or decentralized planning. On the other hand,

I hope that those on the New Left will not be put off by Lindbeck's occasional tart critiques. De Tocqueville's strictures on America were at first resented, particularly where his shafts went to the heart; but in the end we gained more from his work than did the supercilious Europeans.

When Lindbeck points out that often the New Left manages to be critical *both of the market and of the bureaucracy*, and that it is a sign of immaturity or of sentimentalism to think you can have it both ways, he is as little likely to be as popular with the groups he comments on as Margaret Mead would be if she called to the attention of the citizenry of New Guinea the oddity of their refusal to sleep with their cousin's cousin, or their insistence upon doing nothing but that.

An active member of the New Left will, then, not read the book in the expectation that it will convince him of the error of his ways. He will read it in order to give his views that severe self-testing which, as John Stuart Mill reminded us in connection with the necessity for free speech, is a necessary condition for conviction.

But most of all one would expect the readers of this book to be those who, like its author, have still an open mind on these momentous issues. You don't have to be an econometrician to tie in to this discussion. You don't even have to be a student of economics. No diagrams or equations interrupt this reasoned conversation. To be sure, the non-economist will not polish off this text in the time that he can read *Love Story*. But he will, I am sure, learn more from these hundred or so pages and will be given more to ponder over than if he spends the weekend grappling with the prolix sermons of Charles Reich's *The Greening of America*.

To the New Left most of the currently fashionable economic textbooks look pretty much alike. Any of them would benefit from being assigned alongside of the present work. Just because *Pride and Prejudice* is assigned in school doesn't make Jane Austen a dull writer; just because a paperback appears on a compulsory reading list doesn't make its subject matter boring or irrelevant. I may add that some unconventional economic textbooks, written by those proud to call themselves radical economists, are now on the way. This Lindbeck book will not lose in usefulness in being assigned as collateral reading along with such new textbooks.

THE NEW CONSCIOUSNESS

Good wine needs no glowing introduction. But I think it is appropriate for me to point out that Lindbeck's discussion has a relevance that goes far beyond the New Left itself. The ideas he is examining are not the esoteric views of a small sect of the SDS or of Village bohemians. Every single notion that is fervently held by those revolutionaries zealous to reform the bone and marrow of contemporary society are endemic in the minds of all of our population under 30.

It is laughable to think of John Kenneth Galbraith, although he is often cited by the New Left, as a revolutionary; and there is no shortage of critics from the Left who regard him as an echo of Thorstein Veblen and an apologist for the new industrial state his pen describes. Still, the ideas of Galbraith have an importance today that exceeds any influence Veblen had during his lifetime or since his death. For a better parallel you must turn to the role that R. H. Tawney played in converting the minds of educated Englishmen away from the Tory–Liberal dichotomy and toward a fundamental rejection of the acquisitive society. Alert Americans, before they have arrived in college as freshmen, have already read *The Affluent Society* and sampled *The New*

Industrial State. This helps explain why Ralph Nader is one of the most important men in America today. The fact that he is so is a reflection of a deep distrust of the business establishment and a similar suspicion of the government itself. This is not a passing mood which will evaporate once the Kent State killings are forgotten and a Vice President Agnew stops shooting off his mouth.

It is true that the campuses have been quieter in some years than in others. It is true that the ending of the Vietnam war will remove some of the deeper resentments of the younger generation. But to think that opinions have now reverted back to the hopeful days of John F. Kennedy is as naive as it used to be to think in the later 1930s that, once the economy had gotten its second wind following a malignant depression, the American mind had returned to the verities of Calvin Coolidge and Alfred Sloan.

Look at Lindbeck's contents page and purge your mind from any interest in the New Left as such. Concern about the quality of life is not the monopoly of a radical fringe. Or consider that tendency to reject both bureaucracy and the market as coordinator of resource allocation. Whatever its consistency, this strikes a resonant response all across the political spectrum. When Professor Lindbeck points out that the most elementary tools of supply and demand will correctly predict the inequities and inefficiencies to be expected from rent controls in the city, he will raise the hackles of every college student in the land— which is all the more reason why he should be read. When Lindbeck points out that Galbraith's model of quasi-absolute corporation monarchs, who tell us what to want and buy, lacks a determinative theory of how this one particular group of 200 giants happened to stake out claims to the areas they inhabit, the orthodox general-equilibrium theorist must hang his head in shame that he had not paid the

Galbraith system the compliment of taking it sufficiently seriously to have noted this lacuna in it; and, of course, no Marxian methodologist will be fobbed off with a model that simply has some group or agents having the ability to get what they *want* to get.

I could go on pointing out new insights that Lindbeck has put forth. And since no two people can be expected to give the same emphases in fields that are controversial and subtle, I daresay I could differ with some of the author's judgments—strictures against the critics that strike me as too strong, concessions to their arguments that strike me as gratuitous. Such tasks can be left to the future, to those polemicists who will spring up from both the Right and the Left to denounce the author for his findings.

Let me merely conclude by calling attention to Lindbeck's important discernment that one of the most notable things that is new about the New Left is its dominance by what may be called the university mentality—by youth. But before doing so, I think one disclaimer should be made. Professor Lindbeck is discussing the New Left and what I have called the "modern consciousness." He is not at all purporting to discuss that narrower movement which is called *radical economics*. Within American universities today the radical economists constitute an important trend. At Harvard, names like Samuel Bowles, Arthur MacEwan, Herbert Gentis, Thomas Weisskopf, and Stephen Marglin stand for something new under the sun. Elsewhere, at The New School for Social Research, American University, Stony Brook, Cornell, Stanford, the public universities of California, names such as Michael Hudson, Stephen Hymer, Edward Nell, Thomas Vietorisz, James Weaver, Michael Zweig, Douglas Dowd, John Gurley, James O'Connor, Robert Fitch, and Mary Oppenheimer represent to one familiar with the domestic scene in academia a serious research movement from which much will be heard in the future. The fact that other leading universities do not have members of the URPE on their mastheads does not mean that at those universities there is not among the students, both graduate and undergraduate, a growing interest in alternative economics to that of the standard textbooks. Since the time of Professor Lindbeck's visiting professorship in America, this movement has grown in numbers and importance. It was appropriate, however, for Professor Lindbeck to desist from judging a research effort that is just beginning; later, when the fruits of these studies begin to pile up, it will be inexcusable if the American economics profession does not give them the attention, and praise and critiques, that their quality and seriousness merit.

FROM THE JUNIOR COMMON ROOM

Who shall lead the revolution? Many answers have been given. The downtrodden worker himself. But not by himself, necessarily: with the help of the intellectual bourgeoisie. Or, in Lenin's reformulation, the professional agitator and revolutionist must be counted upon to shape the spontaneous consciousness of the downtrodden proletariat, sheltering them from the temptations of revisionist reform and cooling off the premature enthusiasms of disastrous utopianism.

Now Marcuses and Goodmans and Reichs have come forward to say to university youth: Who shall lead? It is *you* who shall lead. Upon reflection, the message is found to have merit in the ears of their listeners. Indeed, who is the most repressed by modern society? Who is most learned and least tainted with the rottenness of the older generation? The questions answer themselves.

I exaggerate, but I do not jest. The Marxian strategy of trying to understand the development of ideology and history out of the material conditions of production and class structure of society leads to fruitful hypotheses in this area. Youth, college youth, do not form a class in the conventional Marxian sense; but they do live under conditions peculiar to themselves, with a distinguishable economic base. And all *a priori* theories aside, one must accept the facts of experience: it was youth who formed the spearhead of the civil rights movement in the South. When white liberals were no longer welcome there, the action moved toward opposition, passive and active, to the Vietnam war. The fortress of the university itself came under siege in the name of "participatory democracy." The unmaking of a President, LBJ, was the fruit of work by young people in the New Hampshire campaign of Eugene McCarthy.

There is nothing new about this except in America. Abroad, the campus has always been the seedbed of social change. Korean and Indonesian governments have toppled when students shook the tree. The Japanese are great imitators of Western technology, but where radical activity on the part of students is concerned, and, for that matter, interest in Marxism on the part of the faculty, the Japanese have long been in the van. When the long-suffering students in Paris—now there *is* an exploited group—erupted in 1968, they very nearly brought down the de Gaulle government.

A class is formed as much by pressures from without as from within. Persecution of the Jews helps to maintain their group cohesion. By this test, students have come to form a distinct class. Students today elicit an enormous amount of hate, not merely from the hard-hat workers, but from the populace at large. When those over 30 meet for innocent merriment, their conversation about youth always involves the ominous pronoun "they." Over her third martini, the anxious dowager asks nervously: "Is it true that they smell?" What orgies of sexual pleasure are not imputed to the integrated dormitory life? TV coverings of Wood-stock festivals and Washington marches keep alive the image of the bearded and long-haired barbarian within our midst.

How can students be both against bureaucracy and against the market, the objective stranger asks. The only alternative is utopian self-sufficient kibbutzim. Yes, indeed it is. Students are not out to make the universities like life; they wish to make life like the university, the nearest thing to the kibbutz one will ever know. Read *Walden* and you will realize that Thoreau was able to lead the good life there precisely because the rest of the world provided him with the library books and the sustenance that could not be grown on the shores of Walden Pond. Read Fred Skinner's *Walden Two*, and try to draw up the balance sheet and income statement of his utopian colony. I defy you to show that it can continue to exist as a viable economic entity without monthly allowance checks from parents outside the community.* If simple living and intelligent goodwill could solve the economic problem, poverty in East Pakistan or Haiti would soon be a thing of the past. So it is within

---

*Since writing these lines, I have come across a most delicious illustration of the rentier psychology that underwrites—oh happy word—the Ivy League mind. Dwight Macdonald, that doughty graduate from the Trotskyist ranks, was asked at Yale what he thought of Galbraith's complaint that Reich's Consciousness III was unconscious of its own economic base.

Macdonald: . . . I think Galbraith's reaction ["Who's going to mind the store?"] is philistine. It reminds me of people who criticize anarchism by saying, "But who's going to collect the garbage?" Incidentally, Fourier had a very interesting solution to the garbage problem in his utopia. His idea was to have it collected by *les petites hordes*—children love to play with dirt, so let them enjoy themselves in this way. . . .

Marie Antoinette is alive and well, living in Mayor Lindsay's New York!

the university. The commissary provides the bare minimum of nutrition. (That's all it provides!) Clothing is no item of expense in an era of bluejeans and bell bottoms. Where there is a sense of community and sharing, housing space becomes no problem at all.

But, you will object, many students still work their way through school, in whole or in part. True, but the number is way down: the night school is one of the casualties of the modern age. Even a state university must look beyond its own student body for switchboard operators and maintenance workers. And the places in which the students by and large must depend on themselves for subsistence, by contrast with the elite universities of the Ivy League, serve to reinforce the point being made. I have been struck when lecturing at commuter schools, such as Suffolk University in Boston or the Chicago campus of the University of Illinois or vocationally minded places like the University of Cincinnati and the Rutgers Graduate School of Business, that I am in a different world from my usual milieu of MIT, Harvard, or Yale. Indeed, the University of Illinois at Urbana differs less from Princeton than it does from the Chicago campus. To appreciate the difference you must talk with the recruiters sent out each spring by corporations to interview prospective graduates for possible jobs as junior executives. One of the questions that businessmen often put to an academic teacher is the wistful query: "Why are we in business so disliked? What can we do to change our image?"

For my thesis it is not necessary that more than 10 to 20 percent of the student population undergo a change in consciousness. Most of the world never changes but continues in the ways of their parents. So it was throughout the period of the opening up of Japan to the outer world. So it was in Czarist Russia, through the 1905 revolution and right up to the 1917 transformation: reading the novels of Russian life and the letters of political exiles gives a completely biased picture of what the bulk of the population is thinking and doing; but it gives you a useful picture of what the pace-setters of ideology and opinion are thinking about the future.

A reader of Lindbeck will be prepared to understand how important the movement connected with Ralph Nader has become. It is not primarily hippies or activists who mutter, "Right on," when Nader's legions castigate General Motors for contrived obsolescence through frequent model changes; if it were, General Motors would be much less worried. What many of the readers of *Time* magazine think today, the antitrust division of the government may come to think and act upon tomorrow. Therein lies the power of ideas.

To the reader about to sample the Lindbeck vintage, I say "skoal!"

PAUL A. SAMUELSON

MIT
June, 1971

THE POLITICAL
ECONOMY
OF THE
NEW LEFT

INTRODUCTION

ONE OF THE SALIENT features of the New Left is its intellectual and political heterogeneity. This also holds for its economics. Consequently, it is rather improper to refer to *the* economics of *the* New Left; this movement has no well-defined and unified economic policy program. All that an outsider like myself can do is simply to draw attention to some of the economic ideas often expressed by people involved in, or influencing, the New Left movement, and to discuss some problems connected with these ideas.

The emphasis in this book will not be on the "grand visions," found in much of the New Left literature, of the historical development of capitalist societies. Rather, I have concentrated on the various problems in these societies that are stressed in New Left writings and on New Left suggestions about how these deficiencies can be removed by the creation of a "different" economic system. Most likely, many individuals of the New Left will not identify themselves with *all* of the ideas characterized here as typical of the movement.

Because of this heterogeneity, it is not easy to pinpoint the leading New Left economists. For instance, most writers in the innumerable New Left campus papers and pamphlets —a main source of information and inspiration for this book—do not yet reveal a strong and independent intellectual profile. Among leading European New Left economists, or maybe rather inspirers of the New Left movement, however, must be included men such as André Gorz in France and Ernest Mandel in Belgium, as well as such regular contributors to *The New Left Review* as Louis

Althusser, Perry Anderson, and Henri Lefebvre. It is even more difficult to say who the leading New Left economists in the United States are. However, it is obvious that "old Left" Marxists such as Paul Sweezy and the late Paul Baran, as well as a number of other contributors to *Monthly Review* and other Marxist and socialist magazines, have played an important role in providing a body of doctrine for the New Left movement. There are also a number of (mainly young) economists at American universities, who under the banner "radical economics" want to change the direction of economic research, partly to shed additional light on social and political problems raised by the New Left.[1]

The general attitudes of some members of the New Left movement have obviously also been influenced by Herbert Marcuse, though he has not said much about purely "economic" problems—except for his assertion that preferences for goods and services, as well as for political parties, are "manipulated" by the established power groups, therefore implying that existing individual preferences are not worth respecting. Among other ideas expressed by Marcuse and related to the economic philosophy of part of the New Left, is the notion that workers nowadays are largely integrated into the established socioeconomic structure and that the rapidly increasing numbers of students and intellectuals may therefore form a new revolutionary class of employees

---

[1]For a selection of New Left writings see the lists prepared by the Union for Radical Political Economies and the Young Socialist Alliance in the United States and by a great number of other socialist organizations not affiliated with political parties. A number of anthologies of New Left writings have also been published; for example, Mitchell Cohen and Dennis Hale, eds., *The New Student Left* (Boston: Beacon Press, 1966); Tariq Ali, ed., *The New Revolutionaries* (New York: William Morrow and Co., 1969). Another useful reference is David Mermelstein, ed., *Economics: Mainstream Readings and Radical Critiques* (New York: Random House, 1970).

because they are less closely connected to the owners and top management of large corporations than were the small staffs of white collar employees some decades ago. There is also the obvious influence of several of C. Wright Mills' notions—that a rather unified "power elite" runs contemporary society and that in the future intellectuals are going to play an increasingly important role in social transformation.

Among present-day sources of inspiration for the New Left, it is also necessary to include contemporary advocates of armed revolution, mainly in underdeveloped countries—men such as Mao Tse-tung, Ho Chi Minh, Fidel Castro, Régis Debray, Che Guevara, and Frantz Fanon.

In the perspective of the history of political and economic doctrines, the ideological heritage of the New Left has a much longer background. The sympathy for "direct," nonparliamentary action against prevailing institutions, so typical of much of the New Left movement, obviously harks back to the anarchist and anarchosyndicalist tradition, including Bakunin's ideas about "propaganda by deed" and Prince Kropotkin's rather similar visions. A number of student leaders, such as Daniel Cohn-Bendit, have also looked for inspiration to Russian anarchists and other non-Leninist revolutionaries (for instance, Makhno), who were removed by Lenin at an early stage of the October Revolution from effective influence.

There is also the New Left's obvious general heritage from the "central" Marxist and communist tradition—in particular that of Marx, Lenin, and Trotsky. By Marxist and communist heritage I mean a number of well-known, mutually correlated ideas from traditional Marxist literature: that the "mode of production" (including both technology and the structure of ownership) determines the "division of labor," which is regarded as the main criterion for the division of society into economic and social classes and is thus the basis for "class conflict"; that class conflict determines the main course of history; that the owners of the means of production expropriate a considerable part of the "surplus value" of the working class; that values and institutions, in particular the state, adjust, like a "superstructure," to the interest of the property-owning class; that labor itself has been "degraded" to a commodity which is sold on the market, making "self-realization" through work impossible; that the system sooner or later will be overthrown by revolution because of the inherent contradictions within the system itself (such as the contradiction between degrading monotonous work and the individual's desire for self-realization, which produces "alienation" and dissatisfaction; or the contradiction between the increasing social character of production and the individual ownership of the means of production).

Characteristic of the special brands of Marxism found in much New Left literature is the emphasis on the critique of the division of labor and the frequent elaboration of the related concept of "alienation," both of which are ideas that are particularly characteristic of the writings of the young Marx and his Hegelian predecessors. It also seems that the concept of "class struggle" is broadened, in New Left writings, to refer to a general competition for power between various groups in a complex social structure—a competition in which the struggle of the division of income (the "surplus value") is only one aspect. In contrast to the "determinism" of traditional Marxism, the New Left does not regard as inevitable a revolution of the proletariat followed by the "dictatorship of the proletariat"; among the conceivable alternatives mentioned are a "bourgeoisie dictatorship" or other types of bourgeoisie domination, possibly combined with granting of minor "concessions" to workers in the form of consumption, leisure, and entertainment.

The New Left's preference for decentralization and its vision of a society built on producers' cooperatives with a nonhierarchical decision-making structure, can be traced back to such pre-Marxist socialists as François M. C. Fourier, Pierre Joseph Proudhon and Robert Owen.

Obviously, the ideas about "manipulation" of consumers and voters, with the inference that their "choices" should not necessarily be accepted, go back much further than Marcuse; those arguments are, in fact, rather similar to the classical (left wing and right wing) criticism of Western democracy. Arguments about manipulation are also somewhat related to Antonio Gramsci's notion of bourgeois "hegemony" in the formation of political and cultural opinions, though the notion of *deliberate* actions implied in the concept of "manipulation" was not central to Gramsci's ideology. The theory of "the manipulated consumer" is also consistent with John Kenneth Galbraith's ideas about the formation of consumer preferences by large corporations. In fact, many of the New Left's arguments against advanced capitalist societies are strikingly similar to those expressed in *The New Industrial State*, although Galbraith's admiration for the large corporation and his concrete proposals (or, rather, his lack of *far-reaching* proposals) are, of course, unacceptable to the New Left. Thus, the similarities between Galbraith and the New Left seem to lie in their assumptions rather than their conclusions. There is also a good deal of criticism of Marcuse and Galbraith in much of the New Left literature, particularly of their "non-Marxian" approach and their deemphasis of the role of worker movements in the future transformation of society. Nevertheless, it is sometimes useful, I believe, to use Marcuse and Galbraith as bench marks when analyzing New Left ideas. When "typical" New Left opinions are quoted in this book, they will often be picked from the works of the leading *inspirers* of the New Left, rather than from the works of (so far) rather unknown students and New Left campus leaders. This is the reason why there are many references to, and quotations from, revolutionary socialists of "older" generations— from Marx and Lenin to Baran, Sweezy, Gorz, Mandel, and others. Similar formulations are found in much of the campus literature, though sometimes in a less academic form.

By focusing here on the *economics* of the New Left, a small subset of New Left ideas is in fact separated out and scrutinized in isolation. Not only the general intellectual background of the New Left movement as just sketched, but also its historical origins and tactics—tactics such as those used in its demonstrations for civil rights in the United States, in its opposition to the Vietnam war, its demands for increased student influence at the universities, its awakening of young people to the poverty in underdeveloped countries—will largely be ignored.

Nevertheless, this concentration on one particular component of the program of the New Left, its economics, seems useful, if the discussion is to be substantive and not get bogged down in a welter of generalities.

The salient features of New Left economics are, of course, its critique of present-day capitalist societies, with the important role played by large corporations, and the vision of how the economy should be reorganized. A closely related though somewhat different point is its critique of economists and of economic theory, as it is usually taught at universities in most of the Western world. It is convenient to start with the New Left's position on this latter point, before entering on the main point of the book—an analysis of the New Left's critique of the structure and performance of capitalist societies.

PART ONE

THE NEW LEFT'S CRITIQUE OF "TRADITIONAL" ECONOMICS

OUR DISCUSSION of the New Left critique of economists and economic theory in this part will be mainly "descriptive." I shall also try, however, to indicate to what extent the criticisms are, in my opinion, warranted. I shall try to see to what extent the economics profession has covered the areas of research in which the New Left asks for more, better, and different studies. As will be seen in the later, more analytical part of this book, the New Left's critique of economists also provides useful background for our analysis of its criticisms of capitalism and its suggestions for the creation of a "different" economic system.

Basically, academic economists are criticized by New Left writers for studying the "wrong" problems. Even if the criticism usually is not very systematic, it would seem that the New Left has pointed out five major types of problems which conventional economists are said to have neglected. I shall take up each of these problems in turn in the following sections.

THE TRADITIONAL THEORY OF DISTRIBUTION

First, academic economists are said to have insufficiently studied problems of the *distribution of income, wealth, and economic power* in society. It may be tempting to answer that the concept of distribution has been at the center of economic theory at least since David Ricardo's work at the beginning of the last century. However, I think it should be admitted that, although economists have been interested in problems of distribution, their analysis has often been based on the breakdown of income and wealth into very large aggregates, such as overall profits and wages, whereas the more individual (personal) distribution within small subgroups has probably received less attention. Typically, when economic theory deals with individual behavior units—"microtheory"—the focus is usually on the "representative" household or the "representative" firm, in the Marshallian tradition, which, incidentally, makes perfect sense when microtheory is used basically as a building block for analysis of the economy as a whole, that is, for macrotheory.

It must also be pointed out that problems of the personal distribution of income were analyzed quite extensively in the older literature of economics—for instance, during the first two decades of this century—particularly in Pareto's writings and in connection with the theory and policy of taxation and public finance. As a general statement, however, I think it is safe to say that the development of the theory and analysis of distribution problems has been considerably weaker than the development in many other branches of economics *during the period since World War II*, when problems concerning economic stability, growth, and efficiency have received more attention.

It is probably also fair to say that "academic" economic theories of the distribution of income are still based on the marginal productivity analysis—and hence on demand–supply models—though somewhat modified by such institutional considerations as the influence of labor market organizations, monopolistic practices in commodity and labor markets, and income redistribution by government. This means, of course, that the distribution of income (before taxes and government transfers) is assumed to be determined mainly by the marginal products of the various factors of production and by the ownership of those factors

—labor, "human capital," physical capital, and financial assets—in society.

It is not clear if, and to what extent, the suggestions implied in the New Left's criticisms of current distribution analysis differ very much from this approach. It does seem, however, that the emphasis in New Left writings is more on institutional arrangements and on the role of notions of the "distribution of power" and the "class struggle" in explaining the distribution of income. Among New Left writers with a formal training in economic theory there also seems to be an interest in alternative macroeconomic theories of distribution associated with such critics of marginal-productivity theories as Joan Robinson and Nicholas Kaldor. Until such alternative approaches have been developed rigorously and subjected to serious empirical research, it is difficult to claim "superiority" for such models as compared to traditional academic theories of distribution. Often it seems that the New Left exposition of distribution problems is based on some version of a Marxian labor theory of value with the notion that labor is the only factor of production (or that all other factors can be "derived" from labor) and that a considerable part of the surplus value is expropriated by the capitalists.

In my opinion, a valid New Left criticism of the traditional theory of income distribution is its typically "static" nature. Economists have, in fact, generally not studied the "dynamic" socioeconomic processes very deeply over long periods of time during which the productivity of different individuals is *changed* (by schooling, by on-the-job training, as well as by the influence of the whole environment on the individual); they have also largely neglected the development of the distribution of capital over time (for instance, through the system of inheritance). However, it does seem that just these problems have in recent years beer studied more and more by academic economists, such as Gary Becker and Jacob Mincer, to mention just two examples, rather than from the critical stance of the New Leftists.

TRADITIONAL EMPHASIS ON RESOURCE ALLOCATION WITH GIVEN TASTES

A second type of New Left criticism of conventional economics is that economists tend to utilize too partial an approach in their analysis of problems of the allocation of production factors among different production sectors, that is, to the problems of the *allocation of resources*. In particular, economists are criticized for taking household preferences mainly as given, thereby leaving investigation of the formation of such preferences to other disciplines, such as sociology, which has in fact meant that today very little is known about the formation of preferences that is useful for economic analysis. When looking at the research literature on the formation of preferences, including the effects of advertising and the influence of interpersonal relations on these preferences, it is quite obvious that the literature is basically weak in comparison with other areas in economics. It does, therefore, seem that this criticism is well grounded, though this area of research may prove a particularly difficult one, and it should not be forgotten that it was an economist—Thorstein Veblen—who first made an important point of the formation of preferences—the "Veblen effect."

In fact, it is not quite clear how effective research in this field can be carried out. Some New Left writers obviously regard theories about "bourgeoisie domination" and "manipulation" of institutions, values, and preferences as the natural approach to the study of the problem of the formation of preferences. This, of course, fits in quite well with the Marxist theory of the development of a "superstr cture" of institutions serving the interests of capitalists and with, for instance, Gramsci's theory of bourgeoisie domination.

Most social scientists presumably want more flexible and "open-minded" studies of the extremely complex mechanisms by which values and preferences are formed and changed in present-day societies. The activities of large corporations, of dominant groups of property owners, of the military establishment, and the political leaders may, of course, be important subjects of such studies—together with studies of the role of labor-union leaders, minority groups, and various protest groups, including the New Left movement itself. As long as research in this difficult field is in its present "underdeveloped" state, speculations will presumably always fill the vacuum created by the lack of scientific knowledge; this means that both the "ultraliberal" notion of the basic autonomy of individual preferences and its opposite, the notion of the manipulated consumer, may well coexist for a long time to come.

THE QUALITY OF LIFE

A third criticism of economics, to some extent related to New Left views on the role of preferences, is that the profession has paid much too little attention to problems of the *quality of life*, compared to that paid to the quantity and composition of output of commodities and services. Part of the criticism is that in their analysis economists concentrate on the satisfaction of preferences for consumer goods, and possibly for leisure time, thus partly neglecting such problems as working conditions, the ways in which decisions are made, and the problem of the quality of the general environment, natural as well as man-made—basically, problems related to the "externalities" of production and consumption.

Sometimes this criticism, too, is given a Marxist flavor,

by tying it to Marxist notions of the "obsession" of capitalists with the accumulation of capital and the "unlimited" expansion of production, regardless of other values in society. Deterioration of the environment, alienation in work, and neglect of collective services are thus seen as unavoidable characteristics of a capitalist society; increased profits and GNP are said to be the dominating indexes of and incentives for capitalist "development."

In defense of economists on this point, it may be argued that economic theory has dealt quite extensively with problems of "external effects," such as pollution and city blight, extensively enough even to constitute a foundation for policy action, at least since the classical treatment of welfare economics by Pigou at the time of World War I. Thus, in this field traditional economists no doubt have an acceptable theory to explain environmental deterioration: the theory of "external" effects, which shows how a nonoptimal allocation of resources emerges when the productive activities of individual firms and the consumption of individual households influence the production process in other firms or the well-being of other households. There is also an interesting and rapidly growing literature in which various methods (like tax-subsidy programs) of dealing with externalities are analyzed.

There also exists a considerable literature in labor economics and social insurance—a literature in which relations between economic and social conditions are analyzed closely. I think it must be admitted, however, that there has been a tendency for the externalities to slip down to the footnotes, particularly in our textbooks, and that social conditions have hardly been at the center of the analysis in economic textbooks.

One reason for the neglect of the external effects of modern technology on our environment is probably that until recently we did not have much information about the enormous dimensions of these externalities. It is also quite likely that these conditions—in the form of air, water, and land pollution—have increased drastically during recent decades. Perhaps the environment is also a "luxury good," in the sense that people do not give high priority to the environment until their standard of living in terms of consumption goods has reached a rather substantial level. It does seem, however, that air, water, and land pollution now has reached such dimensions that countries with low standards of living probably also now have reason to be concerned about some of the external effects on the natural and man-made environment. In fact, this problem has ceased to be national and has become international in scope.

It is thus high time that a dynamic version of the Walrasian general-equilibrium system of economic analysis be related to the ecological equilibrium system of our natural environment, as well as to the man-made environmental system. Blame for the neglect of externality problems in practical policy in all countries should, of course, be laid not only at the door of economists. Politicians and the electorate are more to blame than economic theorists. After all, far-reaching suggestions for action against external effects on our environment have been constantly offered by natural and social scientists for at least a decade.

LARGE VERSUS SMALL CHANGES

A fourth criticism of traditional economics by the New Left is that the economists are obsessed with *marginal changes* within a given economic system—that they study the effects of small parameter shifts, susceptible to analysis by differential calculus, rather than discuss large, *qualitative changes* in the economic system. In other words, economists are criticized for confining their studies mainly to "local optima," in the neighborhood of the initial position, rather than asking whether there may be some superior "total optimum" position in a society organized quite differently from those we know. Occasionally, marginal analysis is even labeled "antirevolutionary."

This criticism is, of course, related to the assertion that the analysis of the allocation of resources utilizes too partial an approach, for instance, by not studying sufficiently the formation of preferences. Here, too, the criticism is given a Marxian touch by the New Left when they emphasize the need for the study of great historic processes and transformations of systems when their inherent "contradictions" become too strong.

Thus, economists are in fact criticized for neglect of the important but difficult fields of "comparative economic systems." To quote Marcuse: "In order to identify and define the possibilities of an optimal development, the critical theory must abstract from the actual organization and utilization of society's resources. . . ."[1]

I think that this type of criticism of the economists' choice of research topics makes perfectly good sense. The literature on comparative economic systems is not among the strongest in economics. However, there have unquestionably been important contributions to some areas of this field, particularly on a rather abstract theoretical level, sometimes using analytical techniques which make the field difficult for laymen to grasp. For instance, the vast literature on market systems and the differences between centralization and decentralization must be regarded as a significant achievement in the field of comparative economic systems.

[1]Herbert Marcuse, *One Dimensional Man* (Boston: Beacon Press, 1964), p. xi.

The same is true of the literature on different market forms, on laissez faire policy versus "Keynesian" policy, on the role of price flexibility, and so on.

THE ROLE OF POLITICAL CONSIDERATIONS

Finally, the New Left criticizes economists for having neglected problems of the *interaction between economic and political factors.* In particular, economists are said to have avoided problems of the distribution of power in the economy along with its implications for both domestic and foreign policies. In particular, economists are charged with having tended to suggest that there is some sort of "social balance" and "harmony" in society, thereby concealing such phenomena as the conflicts and power struggles of individuals, groups, and classes. For instance, the use of equilibrium models in economic analysis is criticized as a means of avoiding problems of conflicts and "disharmony." This criticism, too, is sometimes formulated in Marxist terms when the New Left evokes the notion of an "inevitable" class struggle and condemns the emergence of political institutions designed to maintain capitalist exploitation of workers and bourgeoisie domination, in order to conserve the basic power structure of society.

With respect to *domestic* policy, the criticism seems to be mainly that economists have not studied sufficiently enough the activities of economically and politically strong and well-organized classes and pressure groups. They have not examined the self-serving influence of these groups on legislation and public administration at the expense of underprivileged minority groups. I believe there is substance in this criticism. To some extent the lack of analysis of the behavior of interest groups may be a result of the tendency in economic theory to regard individual households and firms, rather than organized groups, as the crucial behavior units. There are, of course, a number of isolated studies of how, for instance, various types of economic regulation (of railways, oil production, radio and television, and so on) and tax legislation (loopholes) favor certain well-established and affluent groups in various countries. However, we still lack more comprehensive attempts at an overall view, partly because many important fields are still hardly penetrated by empirical analysis.

Where it concerns *foreign* policy, the criticism seems to be mainly that traditional economists, in contrast to Marxist economists, have not studied sufficiently how developed countries obtain economic, social, political, and cultural influence in other countries. They have not considered deeply enough the role of foreign investment, foreign aid, trade policies, military commitments, and general foreign-policy action (among which many individual actions may be largely beneficial to the "receiving" countries). In sum, economists have too much neglected the problem of foreign domination and imperialism.

There is, of course, an old economic theory of imperialism emanating from Marx and developed by such authors as Lenin, Rosa Luxemburg, and Rudolf Hilferding. It is built on the assumption that capitalist countries need military spending or a foreign "outlet," in the form of investment abroad, for excess domestic saving, in order to avoid mass unemployment. Certainly, this theory seems rather obsolete in view of the postwar economic experience, which has indicated that there is a permanent tendency for domestic saving to fall short of investment—with excess demand, low unemployment, and inflationary tendencies as results. This has been the general experience even in countries with very small military spending and insignificant foreign investment, such as Japan and West Germany. This seems to indicate that foreign investment, heavy military spending, and an aggressive foreign policy are not necessary for a high level of capacity utilization in capitalist countries.

On a theoretical level, the Marxist theory of imperialism can be said to have been made obsolete by the Keynesian revolution, which taught us how to maintain a high level of employment through deliberate "demand management," mainly by means of monetary and fiscal policy. Attempts at more realistic reformulations (for instance, by Harry Magdoff) have hardly removed, or even tried to remove, the basic weakness of the Marxian model of imperialism, though it has been suggested by Magdoff and others, that interest in a guaranteed supply of raw materials presumably might be a partial explanation for the foreign policies of such countries as the United States and the Soviet Union. However, these are general, common-sence considerations, which are not closely tied to the Marxist theory of imperialism—or to "ordinary" economic theory, for that matter. The same seems to hold for A. G. Frank's idea that powerful economic centers have a tendency to pull factors of production (particularly financial capital) from weak, peripheral areas, thus perpetuating or even increasing differences in economic power.

There is also a "new" theory of imperialism and militarism which seems somewhat more realistic than the old Marxist analysis—the theory of Pentagonism, as formulated by the former President of the Dominican Republic, Juan Bosch. According to Bosch, the main problem is not that capitalists in rich countries "exploit" workers in foreign countries, but rather that the "military-industrial complex" in certain rich countries, such as the United States, succeeds by means of propaganda and misleading information in allocating a substantial part of the domestic resources for military purposes. Thus, it is mainly the domestic population outside the military-industrial complex, rather than the foreigner, which is exploited, in the sense that it is denied private or public consumption opportunities which would otherwise be available. According to this theory, the military-industrial complex—consisting not only of military establishments and military-oriented industries but also of labor unions and residents in areas dependent on defense contracts—has an interest in a permanent cold war, possibly kept alive by some minor "hot" wars from time to time. Let this theory of imperialism be called "the Eisenhower-Bosch theory of the military-industrial complex." To some extent it probably conflicts with the orthodox Marxist theory of imperialism, for the latter implies that employment and production are kept up in the "home country" by imperialism in other countries and that workers in several imperialist countries must benefit from imperialist adventures.

Often however, the term "neocolonialism" is simply a label for the dominant role played by big business (owned by the rich countries) in less developed countries, applied without much regard for any underlying Marxist theory. Thus, big corporations are often criticized for activities in poor countries even when, in some respects, they behave against the interest of their home governments (as in tax evasion); they may also be criticized not for *exporting* capital to less developed countries but for *importing* capital from them (for example, from Latin American countries).

I think it is hard to deny that economists have had little to say about such problems, that is, about the relation between economic power and the political process. Thus, the New Left criticism of economists for this neglect, both on the domestic and the foreign scene, is probably well taken. However, in my opinion, these kinds of problems are best studied by means of more flexible and less dogmatic approaches than prevailing economic theories of imperialism offer. What is required, it seems to me, are concrete studies of the mechanisms by which various domestic pressure groups obtain privileges through economic and other types of legislation and of how foreign domination may sometimes occur through foreign investments, foreign aid, trade policies, military policies, and the like. Various economic interests—both private and public—as well as national strategic interests—for example, in the availability of raw materials—should of course enter into such studies.

Even if the Marxist *macroeconomic* explanation of imperialism as a means of finding a foreign outlet for excess saving is weak, there is, of course, often a *microeconomic* reason for individual firms to expand their markets in foreign countries: simply, to increase their profit. Obviously, such attempts have frequently been actively supported by governments in rich countries through political pressure or even military intervention. It is not difficult to find both historical and contemporary examples—the colonialism of the mercantilist period and the "classical" colonialism just before World War I—and imperialism of this type probably plays a part in today's big-power policies.

This microeconomic side of imperialism was assigned a considerable role in Hobson's relatively early writings on imperialism, as well as in Marxist theory, based on the assumption (incorrect, as it turned out) of a tendency to a falling profit rate in developed countries. On the other hand, it seems to be a mistake to believe that the business society generally considers foreign-policy confrontations advantageous to the business community. This is certainly suggested by the declines in stock exchange prices that usually accompany international political crises and the rises that usually follow rumors of peace.

EVALUATIVE COMMENTS

When we try to evaluate the New Left's criticism of economists as described here, condensed to five points and also probably "underdramatized," we may say that it is partly a charge that economists are economists only and not also at the same time sociologists, political scientists, psychologists, philosophers, and so on (or social reformers or even revolutionaries). In this sense, the criticism can be interpreted partly as a plea for more interdisciplinary research—a plea that probably makes sense. Sometimes it is combined with a methodological revolt against technical economics, including the use of mathematical and econometric methods. To some extent the criticism is also just a complaint that economic research is not more advanced than it is, which presumably will always be a safe point of view.

Basically, however, the New Left questions the priorities that economists as a group have assigned to different components of the workings of the economy in their collective choice of topics for research. I think it can be argued cogently that for a long time there has been a tendency among analytically talented people to produce small variations on formal models that have already been developed by others. The multitude of articles in recent decades on Harrod-Domar models, two-sector growth models, turnpike theorems, and so on, are, I believe, cases in point. Many young people seem to have been more inspired by technical-model problems of already published articles than by the more complex and "messy" problems in the world in which we live. The choice of topic has often been determined more by considerations of available analytical techniques than by substantive problems. Presumably, these tendencies reflect the milieu in which economics is taught, particularly in the United States.

In principle, priorities in the choices of topic are, of

course, a matter for subjective evaluation, but I think many people today would agree that "too little" of our best intellectual talent has gone into areas of great economic and social importance, particularly such "neglected" areas as the personal distribution of income, wealth, and economic power; the formation of preferences and the effects of advertising; the role of externalities; comparative economic systems; the interaction between economic and political factors; and so on. Obviously, we do not have to be adherents of the New Left to agree on this!

When trying to evaluate the New Left criticism of economists, it is also important to note that considerable parts of economic analysis do in fact deal with exactly those problems in which the New Left seems to be interested. One difficulty, however, is that the level of abstraction often is so high that the layman does not realize the "relevance" of the problems studied. This seems to hold, for example, for parts of the theory of allocation, the analysis of centralized versus decentralized systems, and the study of the market economy as a system of information and incentives. This means, then, that economists have not yet been very successful in the important pedagogical task of translating modern economic theory into a language understandable to the general public. In fact, it will probably always be difficult for the general public to grasp that basic research and the development of analytic methods are indispensable for the long-run development of social sciences.

I think it is also safe to say that in recent years there have been very strong tendencies to expand research just in those neglected areas emphasized by the New Left. We may mention the growing literature on the return to education (to help explain the distribution of income), the economics of discrimination, urban economics, the external effects on our environment from various kinds of pollution, and the like. There is also an expanding literature on comparative economic systems and on the relations between rich and poor countries. However, the Marxist branch of the New Left would presumably argue that conventional methods of analysis can never cope with these problems, and that a Marxist theory is necessary to highlight the relation between all these problems and the capitalist organization of society. The only way to convince anybody of the usefulness of various approaches to economic research is probably to let each person try the methods he believes in and then let the profession as a whole compare the results. This means that we have to wait some time to see if the new group of young economists trying to develop a new radical economics will in fact succeed in making an important contribution to economic research. If so, I would expect their contributions to be absorbed quite rapidly into the main body of scientific methods and knowledge of economics.

There are also some social scientists who have to some extent succeeded in integrating economic, social, and political factors in their studies. Two of the most obvious examples are Simon Kuznets and Gunnar Myrdal. Myrdal, from his study of the Negro problem in the United States to his analysis of Southeast Asia, has made the interaction among economic, social, and political factors the essence of his approach. Moreover, during the last decades, leading economists have clearly not confined their analyses to equilibrium positions of economic and social systems. Dynamic theory, stability analysis, and disequilibrium processes of various types constitute a very important branch of contemporary research. It is probably true, however, that textbooks still concentrate heavily on equilibrium analysis, presumably because it is easier both from analytical and pedagogical points of view.

It would appear, then, that the choice of research topics

by economists and thus the preferences revealed by the economic profession have already begun to shift in the direction demanded by New Left critics, among others. It would also seem, in my opinion, that the most important results achieved in these neglected areas have, so far, been obtained by economists using a rather traditional kit of analytical tools, though in many cases professional economists may have first been made aware of problems through the writings of nonprofessionals, such as Michael Harrington, or more literary economists, such as Galbraith.

Hence, it seems that the increased demand in recent years for new types of economic and social research has already begun to influence the supply of research. From this perspective, the New Left may be regarded as part of the "market mechanism" for economic and social research, contributing to changing preferences and helping to transmit information from the demand side to the supply side of research. Thus, the "wonders of the market system" appear to be sufficiently far-reaching to serve even the interests of the New Left. Maybe this is what Marcuse means when he talks about the remarkable capability of contemporary society to "contain . . . social change," "to reconcile the forces opposing the system," and to "integrate . . . opposites."[2]

It has often been claimed by New Left writers that there is a laissez faire or conservative bias in traditional economics. Sometimes it has also been said that the social sciences, in contrast to the natural sciences, must always build on political values. Objective research in social sciences is considered impossible in principle (although Marxists often argue that Marxism reveals the "objective laws of capitalism").

[2]Marcuse, p. xii.

It is probably true that most professional economists in noncommunist countries adhere to a nonsocialist political ideology and that this ideological preference is of course reflected in the recommendations for economic policy that many of them make from time to time, *not as economic scholars but as private citizens.* If advocacy of decentralization of economic decision-making and reliance on markets are regarded as the expression of liberalism or conservatism, it would in fact be true that most economists (not only in the West) are liberals or conservatives. It is probably also true that many years of studying economics tend to increase respect for decentralization and markets. I think this is a typical experience of most socialists who have studied economics for a long time. Of course, this does not necessarily mean that they will support liberal or conservative parties. They may equally well be social democrats or market socialists.

But to argue that all research in the social sciences *has to be* subjective and based on political values is obviously a misunderstanding and one that denies the important distinction between positive and normative economics. It is, of course, possible to study the effects on prices and quantities in the oil industry of a tax on gasoline, regardless of our feelings about the tax or about the oil industry, for that matter—an example of positive economics. Subjective evaluations do not have to be introduced until we want to decide whether such a tax is "good" or "bad" in comparison with other alternatives—an example of normative economics. The only subjective element in *positive* economics is, in principle, the choice of topic; in this respect the social sciences hardly differ from the natural sciences, however. The same type of subjectivism in choosing topics obviously is involved when a physicist chooses to study some topic on atoms or a zoologist decides to study the eyes of fishes.

On the other hand, what is special about the social sciences, as distinct from the natural sciences, is that the object of study (man and society) varies so much in space and time and that the problems involved in carrying out controlled experiments in the social sciences sometimes make it difficult to discriminate between alternative hypotheses. As is well known, this difficulty may leave room for subjective beliefs, which in turn may be based on economic interests or ideologies. This means that even theories based on personal beliefs, ideologies, or just wishful thinking sometimes may survive for long periods, particularly if they are grandiose, historic-philosophical visions not susceptible to empirical testing. Another consequence is that value-laden concepts with political implications are easily smuggled into scientific studies, consciously or unconsciously. However, recent advances in testing with the help of nonexperimental data have no doubt narrowed the scope for subjectivity in a number of cases. This means that the "death risk" for erroneous theories has increased considerably—although, it is true, the grandiose historic-philosophical visions have not been much affected.

PART TWO

THE NEW LEFT'S CRITIQUE OF THE PRESENT ECONOMY

WE TURN NOW to the more fundamental part of the political economy of the New Left—to its criticism of the present economic order, and its proposals for economic and social change. Three questions will be posed: First, what are the economic ideas and suggestions of the New Left? Second, do they make sense? And third, what problems are involved in these ideas and suggestions? The exposition may be regarded as an attempt to take a look at the New Left's ideas from the perspective of economic theory.

It seems appropriate to organize the analysis into six categories, each corresponding to a classical issue in economic analysis:

1. The choice between markets and formalized administrative processes ("bureaucracy") as a means of allocating resources
2. The choice between centralization and decentralization in the decision-making process
3. The choice among private, public, and collective ownership of the means of production
4. The extent to which we should rely on material incentives, such as profits and wage differentials
5. The choice between competition and cooperation (or collusion) among both firms and individuals
6. The meaning of "economic development"

It should be emphasized that the discussion in the following sections refers mainly to problems in rather highly developed countries, with a fairly complex industrial sector. It is the New Left's ideas about societies *of this kind* which will be discussed here. However, it is important to understand that much of the emotional and intellectual inspiration of New Left thought stems from their observation of the poverty in underdeveloped countries and from the belief that this poverty to a considerable extent is "caused" by the affluence of rich countries and by the activities of capitalist firms in underdeveloped countries—a belief that is quite difficult to prove or disprove.

MARKETS VERSUS FORMALIZED ADMINISTRATIVE PROCESSES ("BUREAUCRACY")

One characteristic feature of the New Left movement is that most of its adherents are strongly opposed to markets. In the literature of the New Left, a market system is denounced as primitive, inefficient, chaotic, antisocial, unfair, and basically immoral.

One problem with this position is that most of the New Left's writers in this field are also strongly opposed to bureaucracy, that is, to formalized hierarchical administrative procedures. For instance, the bureaucracy in the Soviet Union is often criticized in New Left literature. Ernest Mandel is quite representative of the New Left when he argues that "the existence of this huge mass of bureaucracy [in U.S.S.R.] both reduces the consumption fund of the producers and also diverts a large share of the social surplus into unproductive consumption. . . . The arbitrariness and tyranny of the bureaucracy weighs more and more unbearably upon the mass of workers."[1] It may be possible to make a strong case against either markets or administrative systems, but if we are against *both* we are in trouble;

[1] Ernest Mandel, *Marxist Economic Theory*, 2 vols. (New York: Monthly Review Press, 1968), 2:598.

there is hardly a third method for allocating resources and coordinating economic decisions, if we eliminate physical force. Both markets and administrative procedures may, of course, take many different forms: Markets may be more or less competitive and administrative procedures more or less centralized, with some decision-making by vote, and so on. *Thus, the more strongly we are against bureaucracy, the more we should be in favor of markets.*

Obviously, many adherents of the New Left do not feel that they are in trouble when they are against both markets and bureaucracy. And a few certainly have avoided the dilemma either by choosing markets (as, for instance, Murray Rothbard in the United States) or by choosing administrative central planning (such as more traditional adherents of the Soviet model). However, I think it is fair to say that most followers of the New Left have never faced up to the fact that we must have *some* mechanism for (1) obtaining *information* about preferences; (2) *allocating* resources to different sectors in accordance with these preferences; (3) deciding which *production techniques* to use; (4) creating *incentives* to economize in the use of resources, to invest, and to develop new technologies; and finally, (5) *coordinating* the decisions of millions of individual firms and households to make them consistent, so that each industry produces just so much and in exactly those quantities that are desired not only by households but also by firms producing millions of other commodities.

In an economy without markets or with only minimal markets, an enormous amount of detailed information is required by the central planners. Information is needed on both the production possibilities for all the different products (the marginal rates of transformation between any pair of products) and the tastes, that is, the preference functions, of consumers (marginal rates of substitution).

On the basis of such information, a hypothetical super-computer could in theory work out a program for an optimal allocation of resources. If, on the other hand, the authorities themselves decide on the desired "basket" of final output (without seeking to know and cater to "subjective" consumer preferences), information would of course have to be collected *only* about production processes. An optimal allocation of resources could then theoretically be worked out, for instance with the help of an "activity model" and a supercomputer—with "shadow-prices" for factors of production as a by-product of the solution.

Actually, both alternatives have to be regarded as formidable tasks, not only because of the limited capacity of existing and conceivable computers but also and above all because of the difficulties involved in collecting and coordinating in one place up-to-date information about alternative production processes for millions of different commodities. These difficulties will have to be faced whether queues, ration cards, or equilibrium markets are used to *distribute* the total basket of centrally determined consumer goods among households. Because of the inadequate information on preferences and production costs, as well as lack of incentives, we should expect nonoptimal factor proportions, nonoptimal holdings of inventories, absence of efficient investment criteria, and consequent misallocation of capital stock, as well as a poor adjustment of the quality of products and services to the wishes of buyers. This expectation seems quite consistent with empirical evidence from the Soviet Union and Eastern Europe. In fact, it has been difficult in those countries even to obtain reasonable *consistency* in input-output relations, and it seems that the striving after such consistency has often completely overshadowed attempts to achieve efficient and approximately optimal allocation of resources, including the choice of product quality.[2]

Where strongly centralized economies seem to have been most successful is in the mobilization of underutilized resources and in keeping down the share of consumption in the GNP in order to step up the rate of capital accumulation.

The need to specify a mechanism to perform all of these functions is also neglected by the best-known authors who have inspired the New Left. Instead of facing the problem, they usually propose such formulations as this one by Paul Baran: "a society can be developed in which the individual would be formed, influenced, and educated . . . by a system of rationally planned production for use, by a universe of human relations determined by and oriented toward solidarity, cooperation, and freedom."[3] Or, as Baran has also said, optimal uses of resources in a planned economy "represent a considered judgement of a socialist community guided by reason and science."[4] Others have commented simply that production should be directed toward the "true" needs of the individual and not toward the *wants* expressed in the marketplace.[5] Such formulations are typical of what we find in New Left literature about allocation problems. The Holy Bible conveys almost as much information on criteria for the allocation of resources in an economy in which information is assumed not to be supplied in markets by the spending decisions of the consumers

[2]See Assar Lindbeck, "On the Efficiency of Competition and Planning," in Richard Portes, ed., *Planning and Market Relations*, International Economics Association (London: Macmillan, 1971).

[3]Paul Baran, *The Political Economy of Growth* (New York: Monthly Review Press, 1968), p. xvii.

[4]*Ibid.*, p. 42.

[5]See, for instance, Mandel, 2:608.

themselves and where decisions are not coordinated by competition in markets. Nowhere are we told how to find out about the "true needs" for consumer goods. And what criteria should be used for the export sector (which constitutes more than half of the manufacturing sector in many European economies): the "true needs" of foreigners?

Among the "anarchistic" wing of the New Left, the idea is presumably that economic decisions should be undertaken in about the same way as they are made in a democratic family in a primitive subsistence economy. The ideal seems to be some kind of "council democracy," in which people are supposed to convince one another or in which decisions are taken by general vote. It is possible that such a model would function in an agrarian society consisting of a number of rather isolated Robinson-Crusoe economies. However, it is an industrial society we live in, and the complexities inherent in the process of production and exchange not only call for specialization within individual firms but also presuppose that information is obtained regarding the wishes of millions of individuals *outside* the separate decision-making institutions and finally requires that billions of decisions by millions of different units be coordinated and made consistent. In a system of this type, central administrative planning and markets—or rather, various combinations of these two methods—are the only appropriate alternatives we know of.

Related to this flaw in New Left thinking is the notion that the bureaucracy in the Soviet Union is to be regarded as almost an unfortunate accident brought about by the wishes of the bureaucrats themselves and the idiosyncracies of particular individuals, such as Lenin or, more often, Stalin. In fact, as I understand the issue, the large bureaucracy in the Soviet Union (although not necessarily all the *methods* used by it) is an unavoidable consequence of attempts to replace markets by administrative decisions. If economic decisions are not coordinated by markets, they have to be coordinated by central administrative bodies. New Left writers avoid the real problems of the economic system by not realizing that they have, in reality, to choose between markets and centralized administrative procedures, or various combinations of these two methods.

Among some individual authorities of the New Left it is sometimes admitted, however, that a market system "unfortunately" may be necessary for some time even under socialism. An example of this is the stand taken by Paul Sweezy: "The view I hold is that market relationships, which of course imply money and prices, are inevitable under socialism for a long time, but that they constitute a standing danger to the system and unless strictly hedged in and controlled will lead to degeneration and retrogression."[6] However, even Sweezy seems to have argued that market relations and exchange in markets should later be eliminated: "the evolution of socialism into communism requires an unremitting struggle against the principle [of "equivalent exchange"] with a view to its ultimate replacement by the ideal *from* each according to his ability, *to* each according to his needs."[7]

In general, the New Left neglects, or is unaware of, the development of the theory of socialist planning which was largely inspired by the Lange-Lerner model for decentralized market socialism developed during the thirties. Similarly, New Left critics have not incorporated into their thinking the analysis of the techniques of economic planning in socialist as well as in capitalist market systems

[6]Paul Sweezy, "Reply to Charles Bettleheim," *Monthly Review* (March 1969).
[7]Paul Sweezy and Paul Baran, *Monopoly Capital* (New York: Monthly Review Press, 1968), p. 337.

developed by academic economists in both the East and the West during the postwar period.

In this respect, the New Left is to some extent confronted with the same dilemma as is the communist faction of the old Left, which traditionally has argued that bureaucracy is in fact a result of the capitalist market system, with the inference that the state would "wither away" in communist society. This notion, that the state would "wither away" in a system where resources would no longer be allocated by markets, but in fact by public administrative processes, is one of the most puzzling ideas in the history of economic and political doctrine.

The belief that the need to specify a mechanism for the allocation of resources and for the coordination of economic decisions can be neglected is probably strengthened among those reading and accepting the analysis in John Kenneth Galbraith's *The New Industrial State*. In his book Galbraith does not seem to have considered it necessary to explain the mechanism by which the activities of millions of different households and firms—or even of a few hundred very large corporations—are coordinated in the several million different markets in which they operate. By talking about planning *within* firms, and after having declared the market system dead, Galbraith gives innocent readers the impression that an economy characterized by planning *within* large firms is in fact a "planned economy." In Galbraith's world, it would seem that we need neither markets nor central administrative planning. Adam Smith's "Invisible Hand" is replaced by invisible central planners, baptized the "technostructure."

Obviously, economists have not yet been very successful in communicating to the New Left or to the general public, for that matter, either the need for *some* mechanism to allocate resources and coordinate decisions or an understanding of what work the market mechanism in fact performs in this respect. It seems that the work carried out by the market system is taken so much for granted that most people do not reflect very much about it, except when something goes wrong in the system.

Maybe the most effective way to teach the noneconomist about the issue of allocation and the functioning of the market system is to describe the problems which occur when markets have been more or less removed from the mechanism of allocation, such as, for example, when rigid price controls have been introduced. The general experience of rent control in various countries is, I believe, instructive. The effects of rent control have in fact been exactly what can be predicted from the simplest type of supply-and-demand analysis—"housing shortage" (excess demand for housing), black markets, privileges for those who happen to have a contract for a rent-controlled apartment, nepotism in the distribution of the available apartments, difficulties in getting apartments for families with children, and, in many places, deterioration of the housing stock. In fact, next to bombing, rent control seems in many cases to be the most efficient technique so far known for destroying cities, as the housing situation in New York City demonstrates.

It does not seem that New Left students in various parts of the world have shown much understanding of these aspects of price control, for they have made control of rents one of their main, concrete short-run proposals. After seeing how low-income families in the rent-controlled city of Stockholm have waited in the official queue for apartments for five to eight years, while high-income families always can get apartments through good "contacts" or the black market, it is difficult to see the virtues of rent control as a tool of social policy. Similar examples of the social effects of the removal or crippling of markets can be drawn from other fields as well.

Another way to illustrate the role of market systems is to describe problems arising from experiments with administrative controls in communist countries. Even though these countries have succeeded in generating economic growth, they have also been confronted by very much the same problems that are generated by price control in capitalist countries, though of course on a very much larger scale. They have encountered shortages of commodities and the resulting queues; the "seller's markets" and the consequent absence of incentives for producers to provide quality, service, and the development of new products.

The difficulties of adjusting production to demand considerations in administered economic systems are illustrated by a cartoon in the Soviet periodical *Crocodile*. The drawing shows some 100 men pulling an enormous cart, on which rests a nail 100 yards long and 30 yards thick. Onlookers ask what the nail is going to be used for. The answer is "We don't know, but it fulfills our entire quota of 50 tons of nails." The point in the cartoon is, of course, not that administrators in the Soviet Union are stupid but that it is extremely difficult to allocate and coordinate resources and to achieve adjustment to the wishes of buyers in a complicated industrial society without a heavy reliance on markets.

In recent years as these difficulties have been discussed fairly openly in Eastern Europe and as some communist countries have started to move in the direction of market systems, it is ironic that in Eastern Europe it is considered progressive and even radical to advocate greater reliance on markets, at the same time that in the West young radicals regard their opposition to the market system as an important part of their ideology, *in principle*.

An important point in the evaluation of market systems is of course the manner in which preferences are formed, an issue on which the New Left has mounted an attack. There is a strong tendency among New Leftists to argue, as do Galbraith, Marcuse, and some other authors, that preferences are in fact arbitrarily "fabricated" by firms through the production, advertisement, and sales operations themselves, with the implication often made explicit that there is therefore no reason to tailor relative outputs to prevailing preferences. Marcuse, for instance, has declared that as long as individuals "are indoctrinated and manipulated (down to their very instincts), their answer [to the question about their "true" needs] cannot be taken as their own."[8] This refusal to accept household preferences as expressed in market behavior is typical of a very large fraction of the New Left. Characteristic formulations assert that man and his preferences and opinions are formed by the outputs and products and that demand nowadays is adjusted to supply, rather than the reverse.[9]

In a trivial sense, it is of course perfectly true that

[8]Marcuse, p. 6.

[9]In the context of the terminology of economic theory, we might say that the stronger version of this position is a new form of the celebrated Say's Law, according to which "supply creates its own demand." However, whereas Say's Law is alleged to hold for the economy as a whole, the New Left seems, according to this "strong" interpretation, to apply Say's Law to individual products and individual firms: firms are said to be able quite easily (that is, at low cost) to create markets for whatever products they decide to produce. It is not clear, then, how a number of New Left authors or those who have inspired them (for example, Baran and Sweezy) can at the same time believe that there is a permanent tendency in capitalist societies for aggregate demand to rise more slowly than does supply, causing permanent tendencies to unemployment and stagnation—this in spite of the assumed ability of individual firms to "create" the necessary demand for their products. The "inconsistency" would be lessened, however, by putting a "weaker" interpretation on the thesis, that is, by claiming that only *some* industries and firms have this ability to create the necessary demand. But then, why do not these firms drive all others out of the market?

demands for products are "created" by supplying the products on markets—in the sense that people would hardly demand products which they have never seen or heard about. People might have general, though vague and unspecified, preferences for food, clothing, shelter, and sex. But certainly nobody would specifically dream about General Foods peanut butter, Lord and Taylor dresses, Levitt houses, and Vilgot Sjöman's *I Am Curious (Yellow)* if these products had not been put on the market. It is difficult to see why it would be less important to satisfy such demands than to satisfy those that are "spontaneous" in the sense that people would want to buy the products even if they were not on the market—if such products really exist (possibly, breast-milk is an example). For instance, practically all cultural and artistic products—from Beethoven to the Beatles—would then fall into the category of less important and "manipulated" wants.

The idea that there are "true" needs, in contrast to the "false" wants that people actually express and that false wants are created by manipulation, is often transplanted to the political sphere as well. Marcuse has provided an example in his argument that "democracy would appear to be the most efficient system of domination."[10] Obviously, this way of arguing is very close to the general attack on Western democracies launched by totalitarian movements, particularly during the 1920s and 1930s.

Is there any empirical material that can shed some light on the formation of preferences and in particular on the effects of advertising? Unfortunately, as was indicated in the beginning of the book, the scientific studies of the effects of advertising are basically weak. If it were true, however, that sufficient demand could be created for prac-

[10]Marcuse, p. 52.

tically any product that a firm decided to produce simply by advertising, it might be difficult to explain why firms spend so much money to study the potential markets for new products. The purpose of such "prelaunch" studies is, after all, to obtain information about consumer attitudes toward potential new products.

Available studies also indicate that most products that product-development departments regard as "technically successful developments" are never launched on the market because of negative results in market research and market tests. The scanty evidence available also suggests that a very large fraction of the new products that are actually launched on markets fail, despite often extensive advance market studies. A rather usual comment in the literature is that between one-third and one-half of all products put on the market are considered failures by the sponsoring firms, in the sense that they withdraw the product from the market within one year. Among products regarded by the management as "technical successes" only a few, possibly 10 to 20 percent, survive market studies and prelaunch testing and so are launched commercially. Available death-rate figures for new firms also indicate that a considerable fraction—maybe as much as one-half of the new businesses—go bankrupt within one year. (It may be claimed that these firms are mainly small, with limited ability to influence preferences; on the other hand, available studies indicate that decreasing returns to scale for advertising occur at a rather low expenditure level.[11])

Even if these studies are not very comprehensive, the

[11]For bibliographies of the literature in this field, see "New Product Development and Sale," *Small Business Administration*, no. 4 (1963); and P. Doyle, "Economic Aspects of Advertising: A Survey," *Economic Journal* (1968), pp. 570–602. See also Booz, Allen, and Hamilton, Inc., *Management of New Products* (New York, 1966).

results do not seem to support a *strong* hypothesis about the all-powerful effects of advertising on the overall composition of consumption. On the other hand, advertising may have substantial effects on how consumption of a certain type of commodity is divided among different brands, though the effects of advertising by individual firms to some extent cancel out for the market as a whole. It also seems that in most countries studied the pattern of consumer expenditure is related in very much the same way to incomes and relative prices, despite differences in the structure of domestic production and the volume and technique of advertising.[12] The situation is different, of course, in countries such as the Soviet Union, where the government decides on the supply of commodities more independently of the demand situation. However, the impressive queues for exactly those commodities for which we would expect higher demands in the Soviet Union on the basis of Western preferences—mainly durable consumer goods—indicate that household preferences in the Soviet Union may not differ so very much from those in capitalist countries. Interview studies of consumer preferences in the Soviet Union seem to have yielded similar results.

Statistics on profits may supply some additional information about the ability of firms to control their markets. We know that profits differ considerably both among branches and firms, and also for different products within individual firms. I believe that these data do not support

[12]See, for instance, T. Watanable, "A Note on the International Comparison of Private Consumption Expenditure," *Weltwirtschaftliches Archiv*, band 88 (1962); and H. S. Houthakker and L. D. Taylor, *Consumer Demand in the United States, 1929-1970* (Cambridge, Mass.: Harvard University Press, 1966). See also reference in Edward F. Denison and J. P. Poullier, *Why Growth Rates Differ: Postwar Experience in Nine Western Countries* (Washington, D.C.: Brookings Institution, 1967), chap. 17.

the idea that individual firms can by themselves easily determine their profit levels, as often (but not always) is asserted in New Left literature. It would be strange if certain firms voluntarily had chosen zero or negative profits, while other firms obtain profits of more than 20 percent (of the value of equity capital). We also know that profits of individual firms vary considerably over time (aside from variations connected with the general business cycle).

The exaggerations by the New Left, as well as by Marcuse and Galbraith, about the effects of advertising should, of course, not prevent us from seeing the formation of preferences (e.g., the effects of advertising), as an important and serious problem for *any* economic system. First of all, it is quite likely that the volume of advertising today is much higher than is necessary to supply the factual information that it incorporates. This means, of course, that part of this advertising is "economic waste," possibly amounting to one or a few percent of GNP. Some part of product differentiation, as well as frequent model changes, presumably also represent economic waste, particularly in highly monopolized sectors where the freedom of choice for the consumer is particularly restricted. It is also possible, although we do not know for sure, that a lower volume of advertising would lead to lower preferences for consumer goods as compared to public goods, leisure time, and appreciation of the environment. However, it is also possible that a lower volume of "advertising" by politicians, journalists, and writers for public goods and a good environment would reduce people's preferences for these "utilities." In fact, politicians may to a large extent be regarded as advertisers and entrepreneurs in the field of public goods and the environment, which in fact may be regarded as an important part of their function in society. In some capitalist countries, such as the Scandinavian countries, politicians even seem to have achieved wide public support for a rather substantial level of public consumption. In Sweden, for instance, nearly 30 percent of total consumption goes into this sector. In view of this experience, it does not seem to be impossible, as New Left writers sometimes assert, to obtain a rather high level of public consumption in capitalist countries; for instance, André Gorz claims that "collective needs are thus objectively in contradiction to the logic of capitalist development."[13]

The basic problem probably is this: Why should large corporations, politicians, successful authors, and artists have such disproportionate power (as compared to other groups) to influence opinions and preferences? Or, more constructively formulated: Is it possible to form "countervailing power" to the power of these groups?

The conventional liberal–social democratic answer to the problem of advertising has, of course, always been to fight monopolies, to improve education about consumer goods, to create independent institutes for consumer research and information, to enact government laws and regulations against dangerous products and false and misleading advertising, and the like. Until such measures have been tried on a large scale it is probably impossible to express a valid opinion on their potential effectiveness. However, I believe that nobody with knowledge and concern about fraud, misleading information, and consumer ignorance would deny the need for more countervailing power in this field.

If the volume of advertising is generally considered too high, a tax on advertising might also be an efficient method to bring it down. One problem is, of course, that the volume

[13]André Gorz, *Strategy for Labor* (Boston: Beacon Press, 1967), p. 94.

of useful information incorporated in advertisements, would simultaneously fall. A more drastic step would be the prohibition of all advertising and its replacement by dissemination by public agencies of information on consumer goods. Even if this solution were administratively possible without considerable bureaucratization, which I doubt, it is questionable whether most people would consider such an arrangement desirable in principle, for it would mean that producers would not be allowed to stand up for their own products. Some public administrators would acquire the power to decide just what information the general public should be exposed to—obviously leading to a very strong centralization of information in society. In the political arena, adherents of democracy will probably argue that it is preferences *after*, rather than *before*, exposure to propaganda and discussion that should count. The same argument can presumably be applied to the marketplace, but one main difference is that there are practically no institutions in present society that oppose various products in the same way that some political parties try to limit the expansion of public spending, for example. Information about products tends to become a monologue rather than a dialogue. It is, of course, for this very reason that the need for the creation of "countervailing powers" in the marketplace is so strong.

There is also a strong tendency in New Left literature to argue as if information could be distributed without cost. Typical is Baran and Sweezy's practice of including all activities that provide information, and even distribution of commodities, in the waste account on the economic balance sheet. (From this point of view, not only advertising agencies but also political parties presumably are regarded as belonging to the wasteful part of the economy.)

In the New Left's criticism of the market system, the

well-known market failures are, of course, also pointed out: the inability of a market system, unaided by economic policy, to achieve economic stability (full employment and stable prices); its inability automatically to guarantee social security and an acceptable distribution of income, wealth, and economic power; its inability to provide collective goods and to handle externalities such as various kinds of pollution without deliberate government policies; and so on.

These well-known limitations of market systems create the need for a public sector and public policies, and they have stimulated attempts to build up a Welfare State. *In general,* however, the New Left in comparison to other groups, has hardly shown extraordinary interest in improving the Welfare State. Practical programs for progressive taxation, social security, income redistribution, public consumption, and action against pollution of various kinds have rather been the domain of the liberal–social democratic supporters of the Welfare State. As a matter of fact, it is easy to find a rather scornful attitude in New Left literature toward the idea of a capitalist Welfare State. Sometimes this attitude seems to reflect a critical feeling toward the state in general, presumably partly a heritage from the Marxist theory of the state as a tool for the repression of workers by the capitalists. For example, Marcuse has argued that the Welfare State is "a state of unfreedom."[14] The idea that workers are repressed by the modern Welfare State, a notion quite consistent with the Marxist theory of the state, surely must sound somewhat paradoxical to labor parties in Western Europe, which, though often opposed by the richest part of the population, contributed to the establishment of the modern Welfare State. Sometimes it is striking how closely some New Left criticism of the Wel-

[14]Marcuse, p. 49.

fare State resembles the old Right's fears that increased powers to public authorities would bring the end of individual freedom. This partial convergence of the New Left with the old Right seems, however, to be more characteristic of the American than the European scene. The antipathy toward government is so strongly shared by the extreme (libertarian) Right and part of the New Left that the line heads back on itself and joins a circle, with the extremes meeting. Thus, a pseudonymous writer of the Chicago laissez faire school could, by using a flamboyant style of the New Left, sprinkled with four-letter words, give an image of a New Left book.[15]

To some extent, New Left criticism of the Welfare State may also be a heritage from the classical dilemma of revolutionary socialism, where there has always tended to be a conflict between short-run and the long-run perspectives. If a Welfare State is established within the capitalist society, and many of the injustices and insecurities are thereby removed, how can a climate be created suitable for the overthrow of the system in the long run?

CENTRALIZATION VERSUS DECENTRALIZATION

Related to the problem of the choice between markets and bureaucracy, though not quite the same issue, is the choice between decentralization and centralization. An obvious link between these two problems is, of course, the fact that a market system is consistent with relatively far-reaching decentralization, whereas in a nonmarket system decisions have to be coordinated by some central authority. In fact,

[15]See Angus Black, *A Radical's Guide to Economic Reality* (New York: Holt, Rinehart and Winston, 1970). This tract, which at first reading seems leftish and radical—somewhere on the anarchistic wing of the New Left—gradually reveals itself to be of the Milton Friedman persuasion.

a market economy may be considered mainly as a method of achieving decentralization in economic systems, while at the same time bringing about coordination of economic decisions. *Thus, the more we like decentralization, the more we should favor market systems.* This relation between market systems and decentralization means that much of the discussion in the previous section is relevant here, and so it is possible to be rather brief now.

When economists advocate a heavy reliance on decentralized market systems with competing firms, they usually mention the high costs of collecting and processing information in highly centralized systems, as compared to those in market systems (in which changes in prices and in the quantities demanded transmit the necessary information to producers and consumers). Economists have also sometimes suggested that in systems based on central administrative processes some types of undistorted information may be virtually unobtainable at *any* cost. As regards consumer preferences, this conclusion, of course, follows directly from the theory of the subjective nature of individual preferences. However, there are also enormous difficulties on the production side because of the heterogeneity of products and production processes, which make *specific* knowledge about "time and place" crucial for rational decisions and hence for economic efficiency.

These circumstances constitute a great difficulty not only for central determination of commodity flows in nonmarket systems ("command economies") but also for centrally prescribed prices (as in Oscar Lange's well-known model for "market socialism"). In the latter system, central determination of prices requires knowledge and control of individual product qualities; otherwise, producers of both consumers' and producers' goods can always lower the quality of products whose prices are centrally determined, as has in fact happened in most countries during periods of price control.

A main inference from these observations is, in my judgment, that the possibilities for computers *replacing* decentralized competition in markets in the handling of information and the working out of approximations to optimal allocations, are rather limited. For information systems using instruments other than prices determined by markets are inefficient in communicating such complicated messages as preferences, product qualities, and descriptions of production processes. That computers cannot replace markets in *generating* information (about consumer preferences and production technology) and in *creating* incentives for efficient operation in conformity with consumer preferences is, of course, even more obvious. Clearly, these statements are no denial of the fact that computers can be very useful tools for the kind of central planning which serves as an important complement to the market mechanism in most countries—using data generated both by markets and other processes.

A specific problem affecting centralized administrative processes, designed to direct in detail the allocation of resources, particularly in complex economies, is that these processes in reality imply several "layers" of administrative bodies between the firm and the top decision-makers. When information is "filtered" through these layers, it may be a reasonable hypothesis that most of the information is lost and that part of what remains is distorted, for the reasons mentioned earlier. The more details that are decided at the top, the more serious, of course, is this loss of detailed knowledge.

The problem is accentuated by the fact that administrative hierarchies in reality are, and probably have to be, *pyramids:* The number of persons *receiving* information from below are much fewer than the number of those who *emit* information. Consequently, people at the top of the pyramid can devote only a very small fraction of their time to problems that are analyzed and considered very carefully at lower levels. Moreover, the enormous mass of information and decisions at the top level means that "unqualified" officials in the high-level administrative bodies ("assistants"), in fact, have to make the decisions, even though their general qualifications (hence not only their specific information) are often low as compared to those of the most qualified officials in the low-level units (for example, in firms). Thus, not only is information lost and distorted "on the way" through various administrative layers, but also most decisions may in fact be made by people with lower general qualifications than if the decisions instead had been made at the level of the firms.

Obviously, deficiencies in information and coordination are not confined to central administrative systems. Decentralized systems also suffer from inadequate information and coordination. For instance, in decentralized systems there is an obvious risk that macroinformation (information about the economy as a whole, sometimes available to high-level administrative bodies) is not known or considered at the level of the firm. Individual firms may thus plan according to unrealistic and inconsistent assumptions about the *general* level of economic activity and the growth rate for the economy as a whole, running the risk of temporary overcapacity and various types of macroeconomic instabilities. In market economics this means that coordination of investment decisions might thus be improved by a centralized collection of information. This is, of course, one of the main arguments for some kind of "indicative planning" of the kind used in France, Japan and, perhaps to a smaller extent, in the Scandinavian countries.[16]

These considerations are very relevant to an evaluation of the ideas of the New Left; very strong sympathies for decentralization are usually expressed in New Left literature. In this respect, the New Left also deviates from the main tradition of the old Left, which in general was more centralist in its outlook, with more emphasis on central planning. One reason for this difference may be that the young generation today has experienced the problems connected both with tendencies toward centralization in capitalist societies, in large corporations as well as in the state, and the much more far-reaching centralization in most communist countries. However, some of the "older" inspirers of the New Left have also expressed a strong antipathy to centralization, unlike the more "traditional" Marxists such as Maurice Dobb, and to some extent also Baran and Sweezy. An example is Mandel: It is his position that in an economy which is characterized by "planned bureaucracy and centralized fashion . . . sacrifices are imposed without the victims being asked their views and without obtaining *their prior consent.* Such a system of management is contrary to the principles of socialism, and furthermore it leads to economic results which are inferior to those of a more democratic system of management."[17]

One basic dilemma for the New Left which, however, is not brought out clearly in the New Left literature, is that its strong sympathy for decentralization is difficult to reconcile with its rejection of the market system, which presumably is the only type of economic system that permits far-reaching decentralization in complex industrial societies.

[16]See Lindbeck, "On the Efficiency of Competition and Planning."
[17]Mandel, 2:631.

The dilemma is complicated further by the fact that some New Leftists—sometimes also just those who favor decentralization—often also advocate more central social and economic planning. In this respect the New Left is to some extent confronted by the same dilemma that faced the syndicalist movement, which also simultaneously emphasized decentralization and central planning.

The classical way of escaping, rather than solving, this type of dilemma is presumably to argue that centralization is necessary in the short run but that in the future society far-reaching decentralization will in fact be implemented—an idea related to the Marxist notion of the "withering away" of the state in the long run. (Another parallel is the tendency for most new military dictatorships to assert that the extraordinary central powers taken today will, in fact, prepare the ground for democratic elections and decentralization in the future.) The idea that central planning will be absent in a future communist society, though rather comprehensive central planning will be necessary in the transitional period between capitalism and socialism and for some time during the stage of socialism, is typical of several New Left authorities, such as Sweezy and Mandel. This temporary centralized planning should, however, be implemented with the enthusiasm and participation of the masses. "Without revolutionary enthusiasm, and mass participation, centralized planning becomes increasingly authoritarian and rigid with resulting multiplication of economic difficulties and failures."[18] On these issues Bakunin was, in my opinion, much more realistic than were the Marxists, when he denied that strengthening the powers of the state, for instance, by means of the "dictatorship of the proletariat,"

[18]Sweezy, "Reply to Charles Bettleheim."

would make possible a later drastic reduction of the powers of the state, as symbolized by the idea of its "withering away."

Finding an optimal combination of centralization and decentralization—and of markets and administrative procedures—is, of course, a *general* problem rather than a problem for the New Left specifically. What makes the dilemma particularly striking for the New Left, however, is that few groups in society are at the same time both so strongly against markets and bureaucracy and so much in favor of decentralization (though sometimes, as indicated, also demanding more central planning).

Presumably these "inconsistencies" are to some extent an expression of the heterogeneity of the movement—in that people with quite different opinions have been given the same label—and, to some extent, it is an illustration of the fact that political positions often are somewhat inconsistent. However, it is possible that the apparent conflict between the demands for decentralization and for central planning in some cases may be resolved by arguing that centralism is present today in many areas where it is scarcely necessary (as in the school system in several European countries) yet absent in many areas where it is most needed (as in the field of conservation and externalities in general)—which happens to be the opinion of the author of this book.

A related characteristic of the New Left movement is its advocacy of decentralization *within* firms and other organizations, often formulated as a criticism of the "hierarchical structure" in decision-making procedures within prevailing organizations, and its related assertions about alienation of employees. Many writers demand more democratic decision-making procedures, sometimes calling for "participatory," or "direct" democracy. Mandel and Gorz are among those who have emphasized "workers' control."[19]

In general, it seems that the New Left has made the lack of democracy in present capitalist societies one of the main targets in its criticism of capitalism. Thus, the old demand for workers' control of factories, or possibly community control, now often supplemented by the demand for student control of universities, has been one of the most characteristic features of the New Left's position, often expressed as a demand for "control of our own lives."

It can hardly be denied that most firms and other organizations in current societies have a hierarchical decision-making structure. Nor is it self-evident that these structures always result in the most efficient way of running organizations. And even if it were the most efficient way, there would, of course, still be the question of whether the gains in efficiency were worth possible, largely unknown, losses of other kinds, such as in "personal satisfaction on the job." From this point of view, there seem to be strong reasons for experimentation with new forms of decision-making structures within various kinds of organizations and also to follow with interest the experiments with more "democratic" decision-making procedures in some countries: for example, workers' councils in Yugoslavia and, on a smaller scale and with more limited tasks, in Norway, where in a few selected firms, there have been experiments with "self-managed" groups of workers, a result of cooperation between employer and employee organizations.

Actually, the issue of more democratic decision-making procedures and workers' participation is, of course, closely connected with the issue of property rights and hence the ownership of the means of production; one important com-

[19]See, for instance, Mandel, 2:644–680; Gorz, pp. 40–50.

ponent of property rights is the choice of decision-making procedures within firms, which may vary considerably even without any change in the *formal* ownership of the means of production. The meaning of "ownership" is quite relative and depends entirely on the laws and administrative practices of the respective countries. This brings us to the next issue—the structure of ownership of the means of production.

OWNERSHIP OF CAPITAL

The New Left has a very egalitarian approach to society, thus following a basic theme in the socialist tradition. As among socialists in general, this leads to strong criticism of the structure of ownership in present societies.

The classical (and possibly the strongest moral and emotional) argument against private capitalism and in favor of collective ownership may be expressed by the rhetorical quest for equality: Why should wealth—and thereby also income and economic power—be as unevenly distributed as it is in present capitalist societies? Personally, I have always regarded this as the main argument in favor of some form of socialism. It has to be admitted, however, that some problems of private capitalism certainly are not solved by collective ownership and that some new problems would certainly arise.

Let us first look at some of the problems of private capitalism that are not solved automatically by public ownership. In present societies, capital in the form of physical and financial assets obviously accounts for only part of the total stock of wealth in the economy. A large and growing part of the capital stock consists of capital in the form of acquired education and training—what in recent years has been baptized "human capital." It seems that the return on human capital today is already more important as an explanation for inequalities in income in the United States than the return on physical and financial capital. In most developed countries, about three-quarters of the national income consists of wage income, the remainder representing interest, rent, and profit. Recent empirical studies for the United States, such as a new (still unpublished) study by Jacob Mincer, indicate that at least two-thirds of the inequalities in wage (and salary) income in the United States can be explained by the distribution of human capital. Thus, assuming that human capital cannot be nationalized (provided slavery is not acceptable!), the nationalization of physical and financial capital would remove only part, and probably a diminishing part, of the total capital stock from private to collective hands. Of course, the nationalization of physical and financial capital by itself would have important, not to say drastic, effects on the distribution of income, wealth, and power in society.

The most obvious substitute for nationalization of human capital is probably nationalization of (part of) the *return* on human capital, for instance by progressive taxation. A much more efficient method, in the long run, is probably an expansion of the educational system to increase the supply of highly educated people, thus influencing wage differentials. However, then we are in the world of conventional liberal-social democratic policies, in which various kinds of inequalities in the distribution of income have always, though not necessarily successfully, been fought in this way (or it has at least been proposed to have them so fought).

Thus, it seems that the application of the concept of human capital, developed by economists such as Theodore Schultz, Gary Becker, and Jacob Mincer, has important implications both for the usefulness of various types of distribution policies and for political ideology. In fact, many New

Leftists themselves, as students investing in human capital, are "capitalists" by this new definition of capital—they own, control, and enjoy the return on capital or will do so later on. Every serious study of the characteristics of capital formation—including the postponement of consumption; the return on earlier expenditure; the control of production processes; and the "power" over other people—shows that there is a precise and fundamental analogy between physical and human capital.

Another problem that is not automatically solved by collective ownership is, of course, the distribution of *power* in society, particularly under a relatively centralized form of collective ownership and management. In several capitalist countries, such as the United States (but probably less so in, for instance, the Scandinavian countries), there is an obvious tendency for economic, political, and military power to be concentrated in the same hands. Certainly this is illustrated by the amazing political power of economically strong and well-organized pressure groups in the United States; with the well-known ability in many cases to bring about legislation in their own favor—tax loopholes, subsidies and protection of agriculture and industry, regulation of certain industries—at the same time that underprivileged minorities are unable to obtain good education, elementary health care, and, in some cases, even sufficient food.

It is quite possible that a society with collective ownership of capital can solve some of these problems by wiping out privileges and helping poor minority groups to attain a decent life, depending on the values, honesty, and altruism of the administrators. It is not very likely, however, that the problem of the distribution of economic and political power will be solved. In the case of a centralist solution of the problem of collective ownership—nationalization—we would expect the problem to be accentuated, for then the bulk of economic power over physical assets would be concentrated in the "one hand" which also happens to exert political and military power: that is, the hand of centrally placed politicians and administrators. For instance, though in some capitalist countries today we have a strong military-industrial complex, sometimes stimulating an aggressive foreign policy, it does not seem convincing to argue that nationalization would necessarily make a country less inclined to use a combination of economic, political, and military force to promote high military spending and an aggressive foreign policy. Milovan Djilas, the former Vice-President of Yugoslavia, has even questioned whether we should really talk about such a thing as "collective" ownership, for in fact there will always be in every system some *individuals* who administer and hence control (and possibly also enjoy the fruits of) the capital stock, which in Djilas' opinion is the essence of "ownership."[20]

The problem of the military-industrial complex seems to be part of a larger problem: Who protects the individual in a society in which political, economic, and military power, to a larger or smaller extent, tend to be in the same hands? This problem is obviously already relevant in the capitalist countries. A typical example, I believe, is the supersonic airplane projects in various countries: Who takes care of the interests of the individual consumer when

[20]Even Sweezy has hinted at this view of "public ownership," though for a system in which economic decisions have been decentralized to the management of enterprises and resources are to a considerable extent allocated by "the impersonal pressure of the market": "Under these circumstances *the juridical form of state property becomes increasingly empty* and real power over the means of production, which is the essence of the ownership concept, gravitates into the hands of the managerial elite" (Sweezy, "Reply to Charles Bettleheim").

two prestige-conscious governments, like those of France and Great Britain, cooperating with two big firms to construct a plane in which probably very few people would want to fly if production costs were not subsidized and if those who will suffer from the sonic boom had to be compensated? It is not likely that this problem would be less acute if governments not only cooperated with private airplane producers, but in fact owned the airplane factories (as they do to some extent in France and Great Britain). Similar examples of emerging symbiosis between government and industry can easily be found in other countries, including the United States: the involvement of the U.S. government in the regulation of the petroleum industry, inventory stocks of various raw materials, atomic energy, missiles, rocketry, and communications satellite systems are cases in point. In these areas, Galbraith's notion of a unified "technostructure" is persuasive.

No doubt there is some awareness among the New Left of the risks inherent in a concentration of power in nationalized economies as expressed both in its sympathy for decentralization and in its criticism of the Soviet system. This holds both for domestic and foreign policy problems. In the more traditional literature of the Left which is Marxist in orientation, by contrast, the risks are often categorically denied. Baran and Sweezy have simply declared that "militarism and conquest are completely foreign to Marxian theory, and a socialist society contains no class or group which, like the big capitalists of the imperialist countries, stands to gain from a policy of subjugating other nations and peoples."[21] For people with knowledge and experience of events after World War II in such countries as Estonia, Latvia, Lithuania, Poland, the eastern sector of Germany,

[21]Baran and Sweezy, p. 186.

Czechoslovakia, Hungary, Rumania, and Bulgaria, statements of this sort are probably not easy to accept.

Even when the Marxist theory of imperialism, wars, and racism is not dogmatically put forward in New Left writings, there clearly is a tendency, following the Marxist tradition, to argue as if most bad things in this world, including imperialism, were mainly the result of a particular structure of the ownership of the means of production—of private capitalism. According to Mandel, for instance, socialist planning would, in the long run, bring about "the withering-away of market economy, classes, social inequality, the state, and the division of labour."[22]

Personally, I feel that the correlation between the structure of ownership, on the one hand, and political and social conditions, on the other, is in reality rather vague. Preindustrial and precapitalist societies have certainly been characterized by militarism, aggressive foreign policy, and imperialism—and present-day noncapitalist societies are hardly free of a military-industrial complex and an aggressive nationalist foreign policy! If we were foolish enough to single out *one* factor only to explain imperialistic policies during the last few thousand years, it would seem that the size and economic potential of countries are more important explanatory variables than is the structure of the ownership of the means of production. This hypothesis is consistent with the (reasonable) view that the two main imperialist countries today are the United States and the Soviet Union. This means that an explanation of "imperialism" in terms of "private capitalism" is inadequate: imperialism must rather be attributed to the concentration of economic and political power in certain nations, an illustration of Lord Acton's cynical remark, "Power corrupts; absolute power corrupts absolutely."

[22]Mandel, 2:637.

I would also argue that the New Left underestimates the importance of ideology in the foreign policy of the big powers. Both the Soviet Union's intervention in Czechoslovakia and that of the United States in Vietnam presumably are not devoid of ideological motives—to support communism and anticommunism, respectively—quite apart from the "economic" interests of the two powers. To this, of course, should be added long-term considerations of national security, maybe the crucial consideration.

It seems that domestic political and social conditions too are only vaguely correlated with the structure of ownership of capital. Thus, both the allocation of resources and social conditions—such as the quality of public services and the treatment of minorities—vary considerably among countries with (mainly) nationalized physical capital. Similar variations are to be found in countries with mainly private ownership. Compare, for instance, phenomena such as the level of military spending on defense (and attack!), the existence of slums, social security, the quality of public services, the existence of discrimination, racism, the commitment to redistribution of income, and so on, in different countries with (approximately) the same ownership structure in the industrial sector (90 percent private ownership of the capital in industry, banking, and agriculture), such as the United States and the Scandinavian countries. These dissimilarities in social conditions are partly related to the fact that different countries with the same *formal* structure of ownership, by way of legislation and social and economic policies, have given the concept of ownership different contents.

It is, of course, possible in principle to weaken property rights so much—by giving rights to public authorities, employees, or consumers—that ownership of physical property will not differ much, in terms of economic power, from ownership of government bonds or bank accounts. It is, in my opinion, a fundamental mistake to interpret the rather stationary structure of *formal* ownership in many capitalist countries as an indication that the content of property rights and, hence, of economic power, has not changed much in these countries during recent decades. It is also dubious, I think, to argue as if the distribution of formal ownership were more important than education and political influence in determining economic power.

Of course this does not mean that a far-reaching weakening of property rights can be achieved without various complications and disadvantages. Examples of such difficulties, if the process is driven beyond certain limits, include the risk of unclear division of responsibilities, with a resulting loss of efficiency; strong concentration of power in a small group of politicians and administrators (especially if that group also assumes entrepreneurial and managerial functions); long lines of communication; the risk of heavy bureaucratization; and the like. An important research task for the social sciences—and an important political issue— is the investigation of the likely location of these limits within various fields.

It also seems to follow from the preceding observations that there is some question about the notion, frequently encountered among conservative politicians and social scientists, (see, for example, Friedrich Hayek's famous *The Road to Serfdom*), that nationalization of capital will *necessarily* lead to dictatorship. Historically, the order in which nationalization and dictatorship have occurred seems rather to have been the reverse of that suggested by Hayek. In all communist dictatorships today, dictatorship came first and nationalization afterward, rather than the other way around (except for the Soviet Union, where nationalization and the present form of dictatorship came simultaneously). The same sequence—first dictatorship, later nationalization—

certainly holds also for a number of noncommunist dictatorships with largely nationalized economies (for example, Burma and Syria). There does not seem to be an example of a country where it is reasonable to say that nationalization *resulted* in dictatorship, or that the two had to go together.

This is of course no denial of the possibility that in the future there may be instances where extensive nationalization results in such a strong concentration of power in the hands of government that a changeover to dictatorship is facilitated or generated. To look at the problem from another point of view, it is also quite possible that the introduction of a decentralized market system into a political dictatorship helps to pave the way for decentralization and democratization of the political system as well. This possibility was, in fact, one of the main reasons for the demands for economic reforms in Czechoslavakia during the 1960s— and perhaps also one of the reasons why the reforms were stopped in such a drastic manner. It also seems obvious that the structure of ownership and decision-making within an economy has an important influence on the resources which are available to various political parties for their information and propaganda activities.

Thus, it is absurd to argue that there are *no* relations between economic and political structures. My main point about the limited correlations between economic and political conditions is that the relationships are so complicated that simple generalizations—whether by Hayek or the Marxists—are not convincing. This statement is, of course, not an attempt to minimize the risk of a substantial concentration of power and of a limitation on personal freedom in a society based mainly on public ownership. I think, however, that the more universal risks are bureaucratization, a lack of decentralization of initiative, and a propensity to abstain from criticism of highly placed public officials (for career reasons), rather than dictatorship (in the fascist or communist sense).

Some problems associated with the concentration of power in nationalized economies might, at least in principle, be solved by decentralization of economic powers to the level of the firm. Such a decentralization may, as already indicated, be quite consistent with the New Left sympathies in this regard. It seems that the ideal economic structure in much of New Left writing is an economy of autonomous (possibly rather small), firms, owned and operated by the employees themselves—a kind of producers' cooperative, or "collective capitalism." Mandel talks about "self-management of free communes of producers and consumers, in which everybody will take it in turn to carry out administrative work, in which the difference between 'directors' and 'directed' will be abolished, and a federation which will eventually cover the whole world."[23] A great many such firms were in fact started on the European continent during the second half of the nineteenth century and the early years of the present century. The traditional explanation of their inability to compete with capitalist firms is that they never succeeded in solving the management problems, and possibly also the problems of accumulating capital and finance in general.

However, to make decentralization possible in complex industrial systems, it is necessary, as was already pointed out, to rely rather heavily on markets. From that point of view it is certainly of interest to note that the trend in Eastern Europe toward greater reliance on markets is combined with attempts to achieve decentralization down to the level of the firm (still within the context of public ownership). But we do not yet know if politicians and central

[23]Mandel, 2:672.

administrators in these countries are really willing to give up the powers they acquired in the previous centralized administrative economic system. A dilemma involved in bringing about far-reaching decentralization in economies dominated by collective ownership is that it is just those who hold political power who can decide *if* they want to abstain from this power or not. Under private capitalism, a considerable distribution of power is more or less automatically achieved when the ownership of capital is not concentrated in the hands of one or a few individuals or firms. Thus, a serious conflict easily emerges between the wish to reach decentralization and the desire for public (particularly government) ownership.

Let us assume, however, that it will in fact be possible to create societies characterized by decentralized market socialism, possibly combined with democratic institutions. What problems will remain? First of all, the problems of economic instability, distribution of wage income, and externalities will not be very different from corresponding problems in capitalist societies. As a matter of fact, short-run investment cycles do not seem to be smaller in most East European "socialist" countries than in capitalist Western Europe. And problems of inflation seem to arise, quite regardless of the structure of ownership, as soon as some modest degree of decentralization of price and wage formation occurs. Note, for instance, the rapid rising rates of inflation in Yugoslavia and Czechoslovakia during the experiments with market socialism. Moreover, the ability in different economic systems to take efficient action against negative external effects on the environment seems to be rather independent of the actual economic system; perhaps the most important prerequisite for such action is, in fact, an interested and active public opinion and, hence, free debate.

A more *specific* problem for socialist market economies

seems to be designing ways for individuals to take *new* initiatives (such as the development of new products, new firms, and new production techniques) when private ownership in the sphere of production is not permitted.

If only those who already have succeeded in reaching the top levels of the prevailing hierarchies are allowed to take initiative, is it not likely that initiative will be hampered? People who already have top posts may often be concerned mainly with the risk of losing them, which means, in fact, a high risk aversion; the most efficient method to minimize this risk may be to avoid new adventures. It is not obvious that such problems can be avoided in a less hierarchical system of organizations *within* firms (for instance, with voting rights and majority decision-making for all employees). In this case too, it may be difficult to launch new ventures if on every occasion the majority has to be convinced that a new product is worth producing and a new method of production worth applying. Another complication is the difficulty of convincing the majority in a firm that a plant should be moved to another region or possibly be closed down completely. We need more information about these problems, and this presumably requires practical experiments.

It can hardly be denied that to a considerable extent capitalist systems have solved these problems, as anybody who can put together the necessary capital is allowed to try a project in which neither the managers of established firms, the politicians, nor the majority of the employees within existing firms believe. Modern empirical research on the process of innovation in capitalist countries seems to indicate that technological progress in fact rests on thousands, not to say millions, of individual decisions. The studies also indicate that "outsiders," quite frequently *new* firms or foreign firms, often introduce the real "big new" commodities and production processes into a country. (For instance, how could the New Left itself have evolved had individuals not had the right to establish new periodicals and publishing firms without a permit from public authorities?)

This problem—of encouraging initiatives—is probably the basic unsolved problem of completely (or largely) nationalized economies, along with the problem of avoiding bureaucratization and a strong concentration of economic, political, and military power in the same hands. An area where public ownership is quite likely to result in an improvement, according to usual values, as compared to private ownership, is, of course, the distribution of income from physical and financial assets.

MATERIAL INCENTIVES AND DISTRIBUTION PROBLEMS

In general, the New Left attitude toward material incentives—by way of profits as well as wage differentials— is quite negative. This reflects, of course, the egalitarian leanings of the New Left movement and, perhaps also, the tendency toward "economic puritanism" which is characteristic of part of the movement. Instead, "moral incentives" and, in the long run, the creation of "a new man" (à la the beliefs of Guevara) are emphasized.

Thus, the New Left is not very inclined to use wage differentials as incentives for efficiency, education, and training, or as a method of allocating labor to different jobs. This element in the program of the New Left is very significant, for the only *realistic* alternative to economic incentives may be—and in the opinion of practically all economists *is*—government conscription and hence the abolishment of the freedom of the individual to choose a profession (in competition with others). It should be noted, however, that it is possible (though we do not know this) that today's wage differentials in many countries are larger than what can be defended from the point of view of efficiency and allocation. Probably a more important point is that the wage differentials of today reflect the present distribution of human capital. It should be possible, through a more egalitarian distribution of investment in human capital, to achieve a more even distribution also of wage and salary incomes.

The New Left is particularly energetic in its criticism of profits, which usually are regarded, in accordance with the Marxist theory of value, as a form of exploitation. Consequently, high profits in certain sectors and firms are not considered as a possible sign of great efficiency or as an acceptable incentive for expansion of production in these areas. On the contrary, high profits are considered as a sign of particularly great exploitation, even when firms which earn high profits because of their efficiency also happen to pay relatively good wages (which is often the case). Thus, profits seem to be regarded mainly as a form of income transfer—which it must be admitted is *one* aspect of profits, at least in monopolistic market situations.

Obviously, an underlying notion is that allocation of resources in accordance with profit prospects is not socially acceptable. This position is usually not explicitly explained, but rather is taken as an axiom in such formulations as "production should be directed according to needs rather than maximum profits." Very seldom is it understood that the relevant question is not profits *versus* needs, but rather that the issue is to what extent a market economy based on the profit motive *does or does not* achieve production and allocation of resources in accordance with desired criteria, such as the preferences of the individual.

As economists have long since tried to show, it is very

difficult to find a better *criterion* for efficiency in the allocation of resources, in accordance with given consumer preferences, than that of production being directed according to profit prospects—provided that a reasonable degree of competition exists and that the supply of collective goods and the problem of externalities are taken care of in one way or another (in practice, by government policies). The simple reason is, of course, that profits are a measure of the difference between the value of the result of production and the value of productive resources used. It has also proved difficult to find better *incentives* for moving in the direction of such an efficient allocation of resources and for improving production technique and product qualities.

Obviously, the same observations lie behind the new tendencies in Eastern Europe and the Soviet Union to make profit maximization the main goal, or one of the main goals, of individual firms in the increasingly decentralized market system which seems to be emerging in some of these countries. A parable from Soviet agriculture illustrates the point. Farm labor was at first compensated in proportion to the acreage plowed and sowed. As a consequence, plowing was done more speedily than carefully, and the distance between each seed was large. To improve efficiency, the authorities decided to pay in proportion to the output of the land, with the result that the farmers used all factors of production they could get hold of, as long as output rose, regardless of the costs involved. To give farmers an incentive to economize, that is, to balance output against costs, the authorities then got the idea of paying the farmers on the basis of the difference between the value of output and the costs of production. Of course, this difference is nothing other than the profit. Even if this parable is not an authentic description of the way in which the profit motive was rediscovered in the Soviet Union, it probably gives an intuitive feeling of why the profit level of firms is relevant both as a criterion of, and as an incentive to, efficiency within firms.

The new economic developments in Eastern Europe, particularly the restoration of markets and the profit motive, are usually not well received in New Left literature. In this sense, the New Left may be characterized as rather "pure" inheritors of the Marxian theory of value, because of its critical attitude to profits even in societies where profits are not received by private property owners. From this point of view, the tendency in Eastern Europe (for instance in Hungary) to pay bonuses out of profits to the managers of nationalized firms must be disturbing, as such payments in fact are very similar to dividend payments to managers with stocks in capitalist firms (as long as the managers of nationalized firms are not fired).

As is well known, the notion of profits as a form of exploitation sometimes leads to somewhat paradoxical results. For instance, highly paid employees in government administration and large corporations (without shares in the firms) are to be considered as exploited, whereas low-income owners of small firms with small profits are exploiters. Following this line of reasoning a few years ago, some "radical" students in Sweden found it logical to support a strike by high-income professional groups (including university professors), whereas some liberal and social democratic students were against the strike on the grounds that the strikers constituted a high-income group who, according to their principles of equality, should abstain from wage increases.

Thus, a consistent Marxist approach to distribution problems may, as illustrated by these examples, lead to rather restricted views on problems of the distribution of income, by supporting all kinds of wage increases regardless of how high the income of the particular groups in fact already is. From a logical point of view, this problem might be "solved" by including human capital in the concept of the capital stock; then it would have to be admitted, however, that all problems of control, return, and enjoyment of capital cannot be solved by nationalization of physical and financial capital.

A classic problem for Marxist theory has been to reconcile the theory of pauperization of workers with the empirical data. As was noted by Marxists at the end of the nineteenth century, a theory proclaiming an *absolute* reduction in workers' incomes over time was not consistent with empirical evidence, which indicated that there had been a rather continuous rise in the standard of living for workers during the process of industrialization. A new theory was developed, therefore, according to which the living standard of workers was said not to be falling in absolute terms but, instead, falling in relation to that of the capitalists—the theory of relatively rising exploitation. During the course of this century, it has become rather clear, however, that available statistical data does not support this theory either, for the shares of profits and wages in the national income seem to have been rather stable in the long run in most of the developed countries studied; in fact in some cases, particularly after World War II, a tendency to a rising share of wages has been observed.

Baran and Sweezy have recently made a new attempt to reconcile the idea of rising exploitation with available empirical data, an attempt not infrequently referred to in New Left literature. Instead of profits, Baran and Sweezy talk about the "surplus," which includes not only profits, rent, and interest but also that part of private investment which is not financed out of profits, plus all public consumption and investment (including both the Warfare and the Welfare States) as well as what is called "unnecessary consumption." Thus, even though the concept of the surplus sounds rather similar to the Marxist "surplus value," it is considerably broader, and more heterogeneous, in scope.

Analytically, the surplus is defined as the difference between the maximum GNP possible with available resources (hence with full-capacity utilization) and "necessary consumption." We are told that this surplus, obviously meant to be a measure mainly of "waste" and "exploitation," was 56.1 percent of GNP in the United States in 1963 and that it has been rising for a long time (of course, the fraction of national income devoted to public consumption and investment has been continuously rising in recent decades in most countries). Many adherents of the Welfare State may no doubt be surprised to find that public schools, hospitals, and other parts of the Welfare State are included in this surplus, along with "waste" and "exploitation." Even though Baran and Sweezy probably are not opposed to welfare arrangements in capitalist societies, the inclusion of these activities in the surplus is not inconsistent with the Marxist theory of the state, according to which this institution is only a tool for capitalists to exploit workers. Similarly, it is right in line with Marxist theory to regard the activities of administrators in the public sector as a nonproductive waste of resources, because this type of labor, to quote Baran, "is bound gradually to disappear as a socialist society advances in the direction of communism" (in spite of the fact that resources in such a society shall not be allocated by way of markets).[24] Some people will also find it difficult to decide what is "necessary" and what is "unnecessary" consumption—particularly for other people.

Another difficult problem, and one that is a *general* dilemma

[24]Baran, p. 33.

rather than specific to the New Left, is that the desire for decentralization sometimes comes into conflict with the desire for equality. Far-reaching decentralization, as for instance in collective bargaining and public administration, easily results in considerable differentials in living standards among regions and possibly also among professions. The centralization of collective bargaining in some countries and the attempts by central governments to influence and finance local governments, can to a large extent be seen as attempts to equalize the standard of living and the quality of public services in different industries and regions.

Problems also arise when Marxist theories of exploitation are applied by the New Left to problems of underdeveloped countries. The New Left has shown great awareness of problems connected with private investment in underdeveloped countries, such as cases of "unnecessarily" large profits to the investors, political influence of large corporations in small countries, and various aspects of imperialism and neocolonialism. I think the New Left, simply by being suspicious, has here seen more clearly than many other groups the problems arising out of foreign investment in underdeveloped countries. However, a Marxist theory is hardly necessary for the analysis of such problems, and the theory does create a number of unnecessary problems. For instance, criticism by New Leftists of investment in underdeveloped countries tends to be particularly hard where private investment leads to high profits, as if investment by inefficient firms unable to obtain profits (or even incurring losses) would be more advantageous for underdeveloped countries than investment in well-chosen projects or well-run operations which, however, result in high profits. In fact, high profits are in many cases a sign that a project is suitable for a country and that the firm is well managed. Instead of complaining about all investments that give a good return, it might be more constructive to argue for better institutional conditions—such as competition and internationally organized advisory agencies—to help poor countries retain for themselves as much of the profit as possible and also gradually to obtain more domestic control of the operations of the firms. Again, profits seem to be regarded as a transfer payment rather than a criterion of and incentive for efficiency. In New Left literature, market transactions usually seem to be regarded as "zero-sum games": What one partner gains is assumed to be lost by the other, a strong contrast to the economic theory of "comparative advantage."

Another instance in which the exploitation theory creates problems is the assertion that underdeveloped countries are exploited when rich countries buy products from them, particularly when the products are produced by cheap labor. First of all, it is difficult, in applying this theory, to avoid the conclusion that exploitation is performed by practically *all* of us in rich countries, wage-earners as well as capitalists—a disturbing conclusion for an adherent of a Marxist theory of exploitation. Second, the conclusion that we could avoid exploiting underdeveloped countries by stopping imports from them is also disturbing, particularly as the New Left often severely criticizes quotas and tariffs against exports of underdeveloped countries on the ground that their export possibilities are thus undermined.

A non-Marxist concerned about these problems seems to have an intellectually easier position; he can "simply" argue for a removal of tariffs and quotas against exports from underdeveloped countries, for the creation of an international tax-and-transfer system to achieve an income redistribution from rich to poor countries (in the same way that has been attempted within some rich countries), and for steps to ensure that as much as possible of the profit from investment in underdeveloped countries stays within those countries—by more favorable contracts for profit-sharing in the future and by legislation to reduce the risk of domination by private firms or by foreign governments (a risk which can hardly be confined to *private* investments).

COMPETITION

In New Left literature there is much criticism of competition—among both firms and individuals. Basically, the argument against competition seems to be an ethical one: competition is regarded as less moral than cooperation. An alternative society is envisioned, one in which human beings in cooperation and harmony solve common problems, relieved from the stress generated by the rat race in a competitive society. This is, of course, the old utopia of both communists and many religious movements. Competition is also accused of being chaotic, uncoordinated, inefficient, and likely to result in a structure of production not in conformity with the needs of the individual. Sometimes, competition among firms is said to be dead nowadays anyway and so not worth supporting.

In contrast, the achievements of capitalist competition were quite enthusiastically described by Marx: "The bourgeoisie has been the first to show what man's activity can bring about. It has accomplished wonders far surpassing Egyptian pyramids, Roman aqueducts, and Gothic cathedrals. . . . The bourgeoisie, during its role of scarce one hundred years, has created more massive and more colossal productive forces than have all preceding generations together."[25]

It seems that today neo-Marxists and the New Left usually

[25]Karl Marx and Friedrich Engels, *The Communist Manifesto*, in *The Essentials of Marx* (New York: Vanguard Press, 1931).

concentrate on the negative aspects of competition in capitalist societies: Uncoordinated investment decisions by competing firms are said to cause violent business cycles; investments selected on the basis of individual advantage are said not to give (maximum) overall benefits to the entire economy; and competition is judged to result in an inferior morale and culture, and so on.[26] In socialist or communist societies, competition is obviously regarded as neither desirable nor necessary. Thus, New Left authorities, such as Mandel, Gorz, Baran, and Sweezy, seem to agree with Engels: "It [communism] will, in other words, abolish competition and replace it with association."[27]

What can an economist say about all this? Of course, we have a static theory of allocation and economic welfare, according to which optimal allocation of resources under certain ideal conditions emerges in a perfectly competitive economy, preferences and technology being regarded as given. There is also a multiperiod allocation theory, in which various limitations of the market solution for investment decisions are analyzed. However, most empirical studies do not indicate that the losses in static efficiency due to production operations below the optimum level in monopolistic firms (the market structure being given) are very large in present-day capitalist economies—maybe one percent of GNP; waste in the form of "unnecessary" sales promotion and model changes has to be added, of course.[28] It is also quite likely that additional economic gains can be obtained in most capitalist countries (though hardly in the United

[26]See, for instance, Mandel, 2:617; Gorz, p. 81.

[27]Friedrich Engels, "Principles for Communism," trans. Paul Sweezy, *Monthly Review* Pamphlet Series (1963).

[28]See, for instance, Harvey Leibenstein, "Allocative Efficiency vs. 'X-Efficiency'," *The American Economic Review* (June 1966); and studies by Arnold Harberger, Edward Denison and others.

States) by a change in the structure of firms to exploit the returns to scale more fully.

I think that this static theory of allocation is useful mainly as a method of understanding and defining the meaning of "the optimum" and to show how very large distortions of relative prices (as compared to opportunity costs) —larger distortions, in fact, than seem to prevail in most developed capitalist economies today, outside of agriculture, public goods, and the environment—can incur very high costs to the economy. However, most applied economists in the field of allocation analysis and industrial organization would presumably argue that the case for competition is more dynamic—that competition *of some sort* (whether perfect, oligopolistic, or monopolistic) among at least a handful of firms creates incentives for resource-saving innovations, product developments, and cost reductions in general. This means that the important thing is probably not whether there is *perfect* competition or not—with individual firms being unable to influence prices—but whether competition of some kind exists (except fraud, predatory price-cutting, and so on), thus stimulating efficiency, innovation, and adjustment to consumer preferences.[29] Personally, I am quite convinced that this is the important aspect of competition. I am, for instance, quite impressed with how changes in routines within firms—changes which are at first regarded as impossible—are suddenly implemented, if a competitive situation forces the firms to do so.

Most economists can probably produce an ample supply of examples of firms whose efficiency increased as a result of increased competitive pressure. Often, particularly in small countries, such pressure can be expected to come

[29]See, for instance, Joe S. Bain, *Industrial Organization*, 2nd ed. (New York: John Wiley & Sons, 1968), chaps. 10–11.

from international competition rather than from other domestic firms, especially in sectors where considerable returns to scale have resulted in a very small number of domestic firms in a particular sector. Many systematic microeconomic case studies have also reported how firms have allowed costs per unit of output to rise when profits are high and how the rate of productivity increase has accelerated when profits have been squeezed.[30] I also believe, though this may be difficult to prove convincingly, that the relatively competitive situation in countries such as the United States and Sweden has been a strongly positive factor in promoting the high and rising efficiency in the industrial sectors of these two countries, in contrast to countries such as Great Britain, France (particularly in the past), and Czechoslovakia after World War II, and probably also a number of underdeveloped countries such as India and many Latin American countries, that adhere to more protectionist and monopolistic practices.

To summarize: From the point of view of economic efficiency, competition has a twofold role. It is because of competition (1) that prices, for factors of production as well as for commodities, are pushed down to levels where they reflect production costs ("opportunity costs"); and (2) that firms are compelled to respond to market signals. It should also be stressed, though it is self-evident, that in principle there is no necessary conflict between competition and economic planning, provided that planning relies mainly on economic incentives wthin the context of a market system, as does the "indicative planning" now emerging in Western Europe.

It is difficult to determine conclusively whether competition has fallen or risen in recent decades. Often the ten-

[30]See, for instance, Leibenstein.

dency to concentration within industries in many countries is taken as an indicator that competition has fallen. It is often forgotten that there are very strong forces that have worked in the other direction. The fall in transportation costs has confronted previous regional and national monopolies with national and international competition. *One* single firm in a country may be in a more competitive situation on today's international market than were five or ten national firms fifty years ago. The gradual reduction in trade restrictions and the creation of common markets have worked in the same direction. A third factor has been the enormous expansion of close substitutes for existing products, substitutes which have, in many cases, decisively increased competition for firms. A typical and classic case is that of the old monopolistic railways, which nowadays compete closely not only with the automobile and air travel but also with the telephone, telegraph, and increasingly also with television. Similar examples abound in various fields, particularly where new materials, such as plastics and artificial fibers, have been introduced.

These observations are, of course, not in conflict with the well-known attempts by individual firms to try to avoid competition as much as possible. Adam Smith emphasized the tendency of firms to collude against the interests of the consumer and concluded that a competitive economy may require strong government intervention to break up monopolies, cartels, and similar forms of collusion among firms. Entrepreneurs are often vigorous advocates of competition in all fields except their own

These arguments are of course not very important for those who reject competition between firms mainly on *moral* grounds, and they are even less impressive to those in the New Left who already regard the present level of consumption as too high. Economists, or other social scientists for that matter, have very little to say about competition versus cooperation *as a way of life*, that is, about the psychological and physical effects on the individual. Presumably, competition between *individuals*, rather than between firms, is not without its human costs, both for those who do badly and those who do well in the competitive race. For instance, in recent years there has been increasing concern in many countries (such as in Scandinavia) about human-adjustment problems connected with an accelerated rate of structural change, by itself closely related to increased international competition. However, competition among individuals presumably prevails not only in economic systems with competing firms but also in administrative hierarchies, as well as among individuals within political parties. It is also interesting to note that when people can do what they like, that is, on their leisure time, they to a very large extent go in for competitive games, such as sports or social games.

However, a society without (or with a minimum of) competition, must also face some serious problems in human relations, aside from the possibility of low efficiency and the relatively poor quality of products and services. For example, it must be difficult to find criteria other than competence (which in fact implies competition) by which to allocate manpower to different kinds of jobs, without using methods such as lotteries, arbitrary command by superior authorities, and nepotism of various kinds—phenomena which also may be frustrating for a lot of individuals. The more the class boundaries in a society are torn down and hence the more "open" the society is, the greater will be the role that will presumably fall to competition between individuals for different jobs. In a society in which everybody obtains his position by inheritance or tradition, competition for different jobs can be expected to be rather small. And, conversely, a "classless society," without discrimination based on race or family background, can be expected to be quite competitive.

THE MEANING OF "DEVELOPMENT"

Many of the previously discussed points—markets, ownership, economic incentives, competition, and centralization—were also at the center of interest for the old Left. A more original notion of the New Left is its belief that present Western capitalist societies (particularly the United States) are overdeveloped and that the level of consumption of the average citizen is already too high. It would seem that this belief is more characteristic of part of the student Left than the (somewhat older), often Marxist, authors who have inspired them.

The idea of "overconsumption" seems to have two quite different versions. One is that additional (private) consumption is, from the point of view of society as a whole, without utility or even is a source of disutility; thus, the marginal utility of consumption is in fact said to be zero, or even negative, though people have not yet discovered this for themselves. The idea is often expressed by formulations such as "it is not true that more stuff is better than less." Or, "the time of scarcity of the means of production is over."

On this point the New Left obviously deviates considerably from the old Left. One reason is presumably that the old Left basically was a workers' movement, whereas the New Left obviously is mainly a student movement. It seems that such ideas are more natural among children from middle- and high-income families still attending schools, for whom the economic problems of raising and financing a family have not yet become a reality. It is, I believe, revealing that though the student revolt in France in May

1968 was to some extent a protest against the "consumption society," when it was followed up by workers, it ended in a 13 percent wage increase designed to permit higher private consumption by wage earners (the majority of the population).

For those among the New Left who emphasize the unimportance of (additional) consumption, there may also be a problem of consistency: If (additional) consumption is so unimportant, why is *equality* in income and consumption so important?

There is, however, a second version of the "overconsumption" theory. This is the idea that private consumption is not too high by itself, but is high in relation to public consumption and to the quality of the natural and manmade environment. Thus, the marginal utility of private consumption is not assumed to be zero—only smaller than the marginal utility of public consumption and of enjoyment of the environment. Let us call this the theory of "relative" overconsumption. This is the idea that the political process has not been able to achieve optimum allocation, that is, a position in conformity with the dominating preferences in society, between private consumption, public consumption, and the quality of the environment. The "quality of life" is said to be sacrificed by too much concentration on the output of commodities and the level of private consumption, with consequent neglect of the externalities of production and consumption.[31]

Sometimes these assertions go very far. Some of those who inspire the New Left have expressed a desire for public consumption to become the "normal" way of consuming. Leo Hubernan and Paul Sweezy have declared, "We must

[31]John Kenneth Galbraith, in *The Affluent Society* (Boston: Houghton Mifflin, 1958) simultaneously embraced both these versions of the overconsumption theory, though without distinguishing between them.

build a system in which public services become the normal, indeed the *necessary* way of life and not the aberration in a few quixotic altruists."[32] It is often argued that cutting down "luxury and waste" in private consumption would make possible extraordinary achievements in public consumption. Or, as formulated by Mandel: "Abolition of luxury and waste, or obvious harmful forms of expenditure, would by itself be sufficient to make *doubling* of useful public consumption in the Western countries, that is, in particular expenditure on education, health, public transport, conservation of natural resources, etc.[33] As public consumption in these countries is usually between 10 and 20 percent of GNP and private consumption about 55 to 65 percent, a rather substantial part of private consumption must consist of "luxury and waste" (if the resources are not to be taken from defense spending, which varies between 1 and 10 percent of GNP).

Obviously, it is not necessary to assume that the marginal utility of private consumption is zero or negative or even that it is low, to argue for the allocation of more resources to public consumption and for improvement of the general environment. Moreover, maybe the charge of "overconsumption" in present-day developed economies often is simply a metaphorical way of saying that the *distribution* of income is unfair—within countries as well as between rich and poor countries. Some adherents of the New Left also seem to believe that notions of overconsumption and overdevelopment are "on their way out" of the doctrine of the movement and that stronger emphasis will instead be placed on poverty (in underdeveloped countries as well as among minority groups within developed countries).

[32]Leo Hubernan and Paul Sweezy, "Socialism Is the Only Answer," *Monthly Review* Pamphlet Series (May 1951).
[33]Mandel, 2:616.

Sometimes the allegation of overconsumption is widened to a charge that today's capitalist societies are in some sense "overdeveloped," an argument particularly often heard in the American discussion. The attempts by some New Left groups to choose "voluntary poverty" (usually for a limited period and with the possibility of returning again, at any time, to the affluent society) may serve as a symbol of these somewhat Rousseaurian ideas.

To some extent it may be a semantic question whether we prefer to call the present society of the United States overdeveloped or underdeveloped when we want to express personal dislike of some of its aspects. My personal preferences are against calling it overdeveloped, however. I would rather argue that the American society has many features characteristic of underdeveloped countries, many more in fact than some other high-income countries. To appreciate this point it should be noted that in recent years it has become more and more common to regard "development" as a *multidimensional* concept, including other dimensions than a high average per capita income and advanced technology in the leading commodity-producing sectors, a definition according to which Kuwait and the United States would be the two most developed countries in the world. In a more multidimensional definition of development, we might also want to consider such factors as (1) the existence of inequalities (for example, large pockets of poverty and undereducation), making a country a "dual" society; (2) the disproportional political power held by certain privileged minorities, combined with discrimination of underprivileged minority groups; (3) the lack of security, both "elementary" personal security in the streets and social security in case of bad health or other personal misfortune; (4) the shortcomings in the quality of public services, such as schools, transportation and recreation facilities; (5) the deficiencies in the quality of the general environment, showing up in city blight and pollution; and (6) a propensity to utilize modern technology for projects that promote national prestige rather than for improvement in the living conditions of human beings—all areas in which many so-called underdeveloped countries are said to suffer. By this broader, multidimensional definition of development, it does not seem self-evident that the United States should be regarded as an "overdeveloped" country, or even a highly developed country. The rationale for claiming that the United States shows many signs of an underdeveloped country would presumably be further strengthened if we also demanded from a highly developed country a "mature" foreign policy, in the sense that relations with the outside world are handled in a nondogmatic way, with due respect for facts and for other people's right to self-determination; that is, if we required from a highly developed country that it show an ability to handle problems of "human relations" not only at home but also in the outside world.

From considerations of this sort, I find it difficult to sympathize with the belief (or, the terminology) often expressed in some New Left literature that the United States is an "overdeveloped" country. Even if it might be more appropriate to say that the United States shows considerable similarities with so-called underdeveloped countries, the clearest and simplest way to characterize the United States seems to be to point out the peculiarities in the distribution of its income and power, as well as in the allocation of its resources. However, it is also apparent that these very characteristics have been exposed to more and more intensive criticism inside the United States itself in recent years, with an increasing probability of substantial changes in the American society. It would, personally speaking, be surprising if these dramatic changes in opinions, particularly among the younger generation, do not have a dramatic impact on policies and institutions in such a free and open society as the United States.

PART THREE

WHERE DOES
THE NEW LEFT
ECONOMICS LEAD?

THE PRECEDING ANALYSIS should have illustrated the opening statement about the heterogeneity of the New Left movement. Its ideas cover a considerable part of the entire spectrum of political ideology, from the most individualistic to the most collectivistic, and from decentralized to centralized positions. The heterogeneity partly reflects the fact that many individuals with quite different opinions have, somewhat carelessly, been classified as "New Leftists," and partly the fact that one single individual often simultaneously holds ideas that are difficult to reconcile from a logical point of view. Of course, considerable heterogeneity can no doubt be shown to characterize other movements as well. Thus, among "conservative" political writers we find *both* adherents of the old "antiliberal" European conservative tradition, emphasizing state authority and bureaucratic stability, *and* adherents of the laissez faire tradition. And among proponents of democratic socialism we find *both* "social liberals," with strong sympathies for the mixed economy and the Welfare State, *and* believers in state control and ownership.

The main source of intellectual inspiration for the New Left has obviously been the old Left tradition, strongly influenced by Marxist ideas, though many of the opinions found in New Left literature are also strikingly similar to those in Galbraith's *The New Industrial State*—notions such as overconsumption and the artificial nature of consumer preferences; the emphasis on externalities and the quality of life; the failure to suggest a mechanism for the allocation of resources and the coordination of decisions;

the notion of an emerging symbiosis between private firms and the modern state; the stress on the increased importance of intellectuals in the production process; and the idea that the educational system is largely subordinate to the interest of the central public administration and the large corporations. Where the New Left seems to deviate most strongly from the old Left's Marxist tradition is in its sympathies for decentralization and its antipathy to bureaucracy, both in the community as a whole and in various kinds of organizations; and, further, in its interest in problems of the quality of life rather than the quantity of output, the tendency in *part* of the movement to be "anticonsumption," the stress on the role of students and intellectuals as a revolutionary vanguard; and, finally, perhaps also in a combination of a rather puritan morality in the matter of economic incentives (and consumption) with often rather nonpuritan opinions on other ethical issues.

However, I think it is safe to say that the Marxist influence in the New Left has increased in recent years (for instance, in the period 1965–1970). This even seems to hold for the United States, where the Marxist tradition in the New Left, as well as in the community as a whole, has obviously been weaker than in Europe. If this trend continues, the intellectual distance between the revolutionary old Left and the New Left may diminish substantially. In fact, many of the intellectual inspirers of the New Left are, or have been, closely connected with the revolutionary part of the old Left, particularly the Communist party. This holds not only for such "heroes" as Mao Tse-tung, Che Guevara, Ho Chi Minh, and Fidel Castro, but also for such writers as Louis Althusser, Henry Lefebvre, Ernest Mandel and Paul Baran. Moreover, the basic feature of the communist movement—the advocacy of revolution and class struggle, in contrast to the "class collaboration" preferred by the social democrats—is obviously also a salient feature of a large fraction of the New Left.

Some of the differences between the old and the New Left may be expected to remain, however, especially those related to the new world situation during the postwar period: the emergence of revolutionary movements all over the "third world"; the establishment of new communist countries such as China and Cuba, which do not accept the previously unquestioned leadership of the first socialist country, the Soviet Union; the rise of Yugoslav revisionism and the new demands in Eastern Europe for decentralization, market systems, and reliance on the profit motive and economic incentives; the criticism of the Soviet Union by communist revolutionaries beyond the reach of Soviet power, such as Che Guevara and Mao Tse-tung; the Sino-Soviet split; the consolidation of a rigid bureaucratic system in the Soviet Union; the tendencies pointing to a permanent *pax Sovietico-Americana;* and the emergence of capitalist societies characterized by a wide range of opportunities for employment, general affluence, and a Welfare State, rather than unemployment and mass poverty.

All these events make it difficult to create a unified communist movement such as that which emerged during the period between the two world wars. For this reason it seems realistic to expect that in the future the New Left will also be much more heterogeneous than the old communist Left.

Depending on the particular aspect of the New Left's beliefs and ideas that is stressed, adherents will wind up in rather different political stables. A schematic classification of these may clarify the issue.

Anarchism. If the refusal to accept organized authority

is emphasized, the anarchistic solution is obviously chosen, as has been the case with various radical student leaders (for example, Cohn-Bendit). The anarchist position is probably most useful in the world of art, where the economic problems of the world are "solved" by symbolic acts, for instance, the burning of money on the stage by the Living Theatre. An anarchistic organization of the economy is, for obvious reasons, difficult to conceive, as soon as we discuss economies that are not the isolated small enclaves of the Robinson-Crusoe type (for which, incidentally, economic theory has been rather well developed, as a pedagogical device in older economics textbooks).

Laissez faire. If a market system is added to the anarchistic model, we are in the world of laissez faire economics. For such an economy a very well-developed economic theory undoubtedly exists. The practical consequence of this position would presumably be the desire to do away with government regulations, to improve competition by subdividing existing firms, and to cut down drastically the ambitions of economic policy and the activities of the Welfare State. In a New Left version of laissez faire, we should probably assume that the firms are owned and operated on some kind of cooperative basis (a system of producers' cooperatives or collective capitalism) or possibly some other kind of public ownership and control.

I do not think that the loss in economic efficiency connected with returns to scale would be dramatic if big American companies were subdivided, for instance, five or even ten times. The average cost curve seems to be rather flat over long intervals, and the experience of relatively small firms (internationally speaking), like manufacturing firms in Sweden, for instance, do not indicate that firms have to be nearly as large as those in the United States to be efficient, particularly as an increase in competition by itself is likely to increase efficiency.

For small countries, the possibility of dividing existing firms into several independent units without considerable loss in efficiency is of course more limited. In fact, it would seem that considerable returns to scale could be reaped in certain sectors of the raw-material refining industries (pulp, paper, iron, and steel) in the small European countries by agglomeration of firms into fewer and larger units. For such countries, competition and a reduction in the market power of large corporations have to be obtained by free trade and common markets.

The important objection to the laissez faire solution is, in my opinion, that we would then have to accept the well-known "market failures," such as economic instability; an unequal distribution of income; external effects which are not automatically taken care of; and various types of insecurity for the individual which private insurance systems will not do away with. If the activities of public authorities are strongly curtailed, there is also a possibility that collective consumption will not be well looked after.

The liberal–social democratic solution. If the public authorities are anxious to fight "market failures"—instability, inequality, externalities, deficiencies of collective consumption—we wind up in the liberal–social democratic Welfare State, with stabilization policy, redistribution policy, intervention to handle external effects, antimonopoly policy, strong attempts to provide collective services and the like. Some public enterprises may be used in carrying out this solution—to improve competition, to regulate natural monopolies, to help redistribute wealth, and to increase the area of parliamentary control of the economy. The ambitions of economic planning, the energy devoted to the achievement of equality, and possibly the degree of nationalization, may serve to differentiate between the liberal and social democratic versions of the Welfare State.

As a matter of fact, the first political program of the

American SDS movement (the Port Huron statement in 1962) can best be characterized as a liberal–social democratic program. Not until later did the movement develop in the direction of Marxism, communism, anarchism, Trotskyism, and Maoism. Other factions in the New Left have all the time been quite critical of the liberal–social democratic Welfare State, with a "mixed economy."

Market socialism. If there is substantial nationalization in the social democratic Welfare State, so that the public sector dominates the economy, we wind up in the world of market socialism, toward which some Eastern European countries *may* gradually be moving, though still without the democratic institutions characteristic of the liberal–social democratic model. The characteristics of this model resemble those of the liberal–social democratic one, except for the structure of ownership (and, possibly, the political system). A characteristic feature of this model is that inequalities in the distribution of *capital* and *capital incomes* can be minimized—in the case of physical and financial capital. As we have seen, however, some problems of this model cannot easily be solved—among them the distribution of power, the choice of goals by individual firms, and the stimulation of *new* initiative by persons other than those who have already reached the top of established hierarchies. In general, it seems that the model of market socialism has not attracted wide interest, and probably not wide sympathy either, in New Left literature.

Nonmarket system with collective ownership. Because of their aversion to markets, competition, and economic incentives, many New Left adherents do not seem willing to accept any of the preceding models. Even though many of them also dislike bureaucracy, nevertheless, they would have to accept administratively run economic systems which, to arrive at consistent decisions, must be coordinated by central authorities. Then we come close to the traditional Soviet model, which seems to have some advocates in the New Left movement, along with Baran and Sweezy, though they all object to specific features of the Soviet bureaucracy, often without realizing that bureaucracy is a necessary part of the model.

Despite its criticism of the Soviet dictatorship and demands for more democratic institutions, the New Left can hardly be said typically to argue for a transformation of society into democratic and parliamentary forms. Instead, the need for revolutionary action by nonparliamentary methods is stressed in much New Left literature. The "dictatorship of the proletariat," for some unspecified time; revolutionary "direct" action against factories, universities, and other institutions; and the seizure of power by physical force, seem to be essential parts of most New Left positions. There are probably also advocates of democratic procedures in the movement, determined to "vote" the community into socialism; this stand does not seem to be typical of the New Left movement, however.

This is not the place for a detailed account of the advantages and disadvantages of armed revolution in various types of society. It is, of course, quite possible than an economic, social, and possibly also (in the long run) democratic development sometimes may be speeded up by armed revolt—in less romantic terms, by "civil war." In fact, this method may in some cases be the *only* conceivable way (within the foreseeable future). One problem, though, is that the human sufferings (unknown in advance) during and immediately after a revolution might not be fully compensated by the gains which may be achieved by the revolt. Personally, I have also always been surprised by the fact that the very same individuals who are against the idea that conflicts *between* countries should be solved by military force, often and perhaps even without much reservation regard armed force as a necessary and suitable method for solving problems and conflicts *within* countries. There does not seem to be much evidence that civil wars are less brutal than wars between countries. Skeptics about the advantages of civil war—a group for which I feel strong sympathy—can also point to the risk that the selection of political leaders through competition in physical violence may not be very "good." Is it not rather likely that leaders emerging as a result of this type of selection process may often be both authoritarian and cruel? The possibility that revolution, in fact, only means a substitution of oppressors hardly lacks historical illustrations.

Thus, depending on which particular aspect of the New Left's arguments is emphasized—criticism of authority, refusal to accept market systems, sympathy either for decentralization or for central planning, awareness of the market failures in the laissez faire model, refusal to accept democratic rules to transform society—quite different political "stables," or parties, may be discovered within New Left ideology. In fact, the New Left is an example of a political movement covering a substantial part of the spectrum of socioeconomic and political ideas.

What a social scientist perhaps misses most of all in New Left literature and its discussions is an awareness of the enormous difficulties involved in solving the problems which arise in *any* social and economic system. There is a general tendency among the New Left to argue as if all, or most, difficulties could be removed "in one shot" by "revolution" or by "collective" ownership or both. As all serious scholars know, the real problems start *after* the revolution or, what from this point of view is about the same thing, *without* a revolution. However, there is very little, if any, discussion in the literature of the New Left about the *methods* of solving the problems which chiefly worry economists, such as the reconciliation of full employment with price stability and equilibrium in the balance of payments; the determination of an optimal growth rate and hence an optimal combination of consumption today and consumption tomorrow, and the manner in which this optimum is to be achieved; the design of a workable compromise between the income differentials needed to give incentives for work and for the allocation of the labor force, and the desire for equality; whether the government should intervene against "persuasive" advertising for commodities; the determination of the demand curves for public goods and services if these are not supplied on a market; whether employees in the public sector should have the right to strike; what the best combination of regulations and tax-subsidy programs is with which to cope with external effects on our environment; how to avoid an enormous concentration of power in a small group of politicians and administrators in a society with growing government intervention; what the best combination of competition and planning is in various sectors of the economy; what effects different market forms have on economic efficiency and the process of innovation; whether a decentralization of initiatives and individual freedom can be preserved in an economy with collective ownership; the advantages and disadvantages of multinational firms; whether important decisions of social and economic policy can really be efficiently carried out by the national state (such as decisions on monetary policy, environmental disruption, and taxation of multinational firms); and the like. On most of these difficult and important problems the New Left is quite silent or superficial.

What, then, are the merits of the New Left's writings? Perhaps we can say that the main contribution of the New

Left has been to remind us once more of a number of eternal problems in the political debate—issues of ownership, distribution of income and power, externalities, public participation, and social values in general—aspects which have sometimes tended to disappear from the political debate during the postwar period, perhaps especially in the United States. In this way the New Left has presumably helped to increase interest in issues of principle and ideology and perhaps also the sense of social responsibility in political debate—even though the questions New Left raises often seem to be more interesting than its answers.

PART FOUR: POLEMICS

COMMENT*

George L. Bach

STANFORD UNIVERSITY

PROFESSOR ASSAR LINDBECK has provided a sympathetic and devastating analysis of "New Left" economics in America in *The Political Economy of the New Left*. After agreeing to participate in this symposium, I read his essay with growing admiration and a sinking heart—admiration as he put his finger surely on central issue after issue, and a sinking heart as he stated succinctly most of the main points I had thought of making myself. Having thus exposed my feelings about Lindbeck's little book, and perhaps my biases, I propose to proceed by stating briefly what I think are his main points, with some comments on them. Then I shall look at some of the points in more detail, adding some observations of my own on issues which may deserve further exploration.

I. LINDBECK'S ANALYSIS OF THE NEW LEFT

After a brief Introduction, *The Political Economy of the New Left* falls into three parts. First, Lindbeck examines the New Left's critique of "traditional" economics. Then he presents a more detailed picture of its critique of the present (capitalist) U.S. economy. And finally, he asks, "Where does the New Left's economics lead?" Throughout, Lindbeck writes with modesty and moderation that may cloak

*I am indebted for suggestions to my colleagues Joseph Monsen and, especially, John Gurley, who disagrees strongly with much of what follows but who has patiently guided me to some of the more constructive contributions of radical economists and steered me away from at least some misconceptions.

Reprinted from *The Quarterly Journal of Economics*, November, 1972, pp. 632–43.

the depth of the insights he presents. He is, moreover, at pains to emphasize the heterogeneity of the "New Left" and to avoid characterizing its position in a simple, monolithic way. And he stresses that he is dealing only with the "political economy" of the New Left, not with its many interests that range far beyond economics. Moreover, it is important to recognize that he writes of the economics of some members of the New Left who are not economists, ranging at times as far as Castro, Mao, and Marcuse. Thus, most but not necessarily all, of his criticisms apply to the economics of the economists of the New Left, who often identify themselves as "radical economists."

Lindbeck finds that the New Left's critique of "traditional economics" centers on five points. The traditional economics pays too little attention to the uneven distribution of income, wealth, and power. It largely takes consumer tastes as given in analyzing resource allocation, whereas the real problem is the domination of consumer tastes by large sellers. It grossly underemphasizes the quality of life, as distinct from quantity of output. It takes as given the social and economic system and concerns itself largely with small, marginal changes, whereas it should be concerned with massive changes in the entire structure of the system. And, last, it grossly underemphasizes political considerations—it should be concerned with *political* economy rather than with the merely "economic" issues that are the center of traditional economic analysis.

Lindbeck has considerable sympathy with each of these criticisms, as, indeed, do I. But they are hardly novel with the New Left. Much of modern economic analysis, in the journals and in textbooks, has been concerned with fine points of professional debate, rather than with major issues of social policy. No doubt too little attention has been given to many of the big issues raised by the New Left, and some reallocation of effort by the best minds in the profession to these bigger issues might well have contributed a substantial net marginal product to our understanding of the way the system works and how it might work better. But, as Lindbeck points out, merely to raise the critical points is easy; the hard part is to show how a different approach could contribute more to our understanding of the operation of the system and to its improvement. For example, the New Left says, perhaps most of all, that we should be more concerned with the issues of power in our society and with the factors that determine the distribution of income and power. But the New Left literature seems to Lindbeck, and to me, strangely barren of concrete, scientifically testable propositions on the relations between classes, "the power structure," and income distribution—or even of concrete suggestions as to how such a testable theory might be developed. Surprisingly little of the New Left literature (only three writers whom I found), interestingly, tries to build on, or test, the sophisticated dynamic income distribution theories of Joan Robinson and Kaldor, who I suppose are now to be considered the "Old Left."

Indeed, as Lindbeck suggests, most progress toward better understanding in precisely those areas seems recently to have come from "traditional" economists using the conventional research tools of the trade. The entire thrust on "investment in human capital," which surely is a major attempt to understand better dynamic forces in the distribution of income, has been headed by such "establishment" types as Schultz, Becker, and Mincer. By comparison, merely to assert that "classes," or the "power structure," determines the distribution of income in fact seems to me to explain very little; only Bowles's work comes to mind as a major theoretical-empirical radical contribution to the analysis. (Incidentally, with all the modern emphasis on the importance of human capital, who are the "capitalists" now?) On the "quality of life," economists like Arrow, Buchanan, Boulding, and Kneese, hardly antiestablishment types, have led the way to date on issues like pollution and externalities. The "traditional economics" has, indeed, not paid as much attention to the political process as I, personally, would like it to have done, but it has far from neglected "political economics." The intensive work of the Brookings Institution group on the federal budget and the budget-making process, and in general on the whole interaction between social goals, the political process, and economic policy, can stand without shame alongside the New Left's assertions that the giant corporations (presumably their executives or owners) dominate domestic governmental policies and U.S. foreign policy, with a comfortable disregard for those facts that do not fit the theory. Lindbeck says that traditional economics ought to do a lot better on such issues, and we ought. He does not find many contributions to our understanding from the New Left economists thus far.

Lindbeck finds the main contribution of the New Left to be its critique of the operations of the modern capitalist system, more than its critique of traditional economics. He summarizes this main critique as centering on six issues.

One, shall the economic system be organized through markets, through a political bureaucracy, or how? And two, shall the system be centralized or decentralized in its decision-making processes? While the New Left is far from monolithic, Lindbeck correctly emphasizes that it generally criticizes the use of markets to organize economic activity —and also the centralization of power in political bureaucracies. But if we deny both, how is a complex economy like ours to be organized? Lindbeck's few pages on this issue (pp. 32–57) ought to be required reading for every student in elementary economics. With moderation, he stresses that we have to have some way to gain information about preferences, to allocate resources in accordance with some set of preferences, to create incentives, to coordinate the decisions of millions of individuals in the society and make them consistent, and to allocate incomes. He looks in vain for the New Left's solution to the problem if we reject both bureaucracy and the market; the best he can find is such formulations as "A society can be developed in which the individual would be formed, influenced, and educated . . . by a system of rationally planned production for use, by a universe of human relations determined by and oriented toward solidarity, cooperation, and freedom."[1]

Similarly, Lindbeck's put-down of the more extreme claims that human wants are now "fabricated" by modern advertising and big corporations is a masterpiece of good sense and perception, not rejecting the fact that advertisers do significantly influence the pattern of human wants, but warning against easy acceptance of overstatements and citing both empirical evidence and analytical reasoning that underline the extremity of many New Left statements. And, strikingly, all he uses throughout are the most elementary and fundamental of economic concepts and reasoning. Properly used, they are powerful tools, and he shows how. There is not an equation or a graph, not an intricate piece of economic reasoning, in the book.

Three, who shall own capital? And four, how shall we manage material incentives and the distribution of incomes? Lindbeck sympathizes with the egalitarian inclinations of the New Left. He agrees, more than I would, that the concentration of income and wealth in the United States carries with it a comparable concentration of political power. But again, he finds much of the New Left literature stronger on rhetoric than on analysis and evidence.

[1]Paul Baran, *The Political Economy of Growth* (New York: Monthly Review Press, 1958), p. xvii.

Most important, Lindbeck insists on facing up to the fundamental difficulty of somehow achieving adequate incentives for initiative in a society without private ownership of capital and substantial income inequalities. He suspects that we can get a better mix than we now have in the United States, involving less inequality and, I gather, a larger public sector. But again he rejects simplistic arguments (advanced by some New Left writers) that all we need to do is get rid of private property and abolish the evil capitalist system, and all will be solved. He writes (p. 69): "This problem—of encouraging initiative—is probably the basic unsolved problem of completely (or largely) nationalized economies, along with the problem of avoiding bureaucratization and strong concentration of economic, political, and military power in the same hands." Lindbeck has a pervading distrust of concentration of political power to solve our economic problems, and he refuses to accept easy solutions that abolish the market without facing up to the dangers of such bureaucratization.

Five, shall we have competition or cooperation? And six, what is the real meaning of "development," and how much of it do we need?

The New Left's argument against competition seems to be primarily an ethical one; competition is less moral than cooperation. Although Marx and many of his followers found in competition and the capitalist state an impressively productive arrangement, the New Left believes it would be a "better" society if we cooperated rather than competed. This argument is closely related to many New Left arguments that further economic growth and "development" are unnecessary and, indeed, in many ways bad. Lindbeck agrees that classical economics has very little to say about competition versus cooperation *as a way of life*, but he asks for evidence that even a "classless society" such as the New

Left seeks could be expected to exist long without the resurgence of competition in important forms. Nor will he accept the proposition that either for society as a whole or for most people in it, the marginal utility of consumption can yet be said to be negative, as would be implied by the proposition that there is no utility to further growth. He finds it hard to sympathize with the argument of some (but certainly not all) New Left writers that the United States is now an "overdeveloped" country, where more consumption has little, if anything, to offer to the people.

Where does the New Left's economics lead? Lindbeck searches for an answer—Anarchism? A liberal-democratic society? A nonmarket system with collective ownership? Market socialism? He finds no real answer. Marx's influence on the New Left has certainly increased in recent years, and perhaps this means stronger movement toward a nonmarket system with collective ownership. Some New Left economists are struggling with these issues. But Lindbeck has grave doubts about such a system. "Is it not rather likely," he asks, "that leaders emerging as a result of this type of selection process may often be both authoritarian and cruel? The possibility that revolution, in fact, only means the substitution of oppressors hardly lacks historical illustrations" (p. 99). He continues: "What a social scientist misses most of all in the New Left literature is an awareness of the enormous difficulties involved in solving the problems which arise in *any* social and economic system. . . . On most of these difficult and important problems, the New Left is generally silent or superficial." He concludes that its main contribution has been to remind us once more of a "number of eternal problems in the political debate—issues of ownership, distribution of income and power, externalities, public participation, and social values in general—aspects which have sometimes tended to disappear from the political debate during the postwar period, perhaps especially in the United States" (p. 100).

II. SOME ADDITIONAL OBSERVATIONS

What is there to add? I append four observations on points that may deserve further attention. But first, a parenthetical comment. The editor, in inviting me to this discussion, suggested that he hoped to get a range of views on the current status of the economics of the New Left; and indicated, with appropriate delicacy, that he suspected I would be somewhere to the right of both the New Left and Professor Lindbeck, who has been generally a supporter of the Social Democrats in Sweden. My credentials to speak for anyone else on the topic of New Left economics are exactly zero. But I feel I have somehow let the editor down, by finding how little different my reactions to the literature of the New Left are from those of Lindbeck. I suspect this reflects not so much our respective political inclinations as the fact that we are both economists—and that the analytical tools of "conventional" economics *do* provide a useful way of thinking about modern social problems, whatever the political tastes of their users. Elementary supply and demand analysis tells us a lot about the likely consequences of rent control laws, whatever our views are on the greediness of upper-class landlords.[2]

---

[2]Lindbeck labels his book "An outsider's view" of the New Left. Stanford, where I sit, is an integral part of the capitalist oppressor establishment, according to the local New Left; certainly it has had its share of campus radicals, and I have done my share of listening to their views. But mine is surely an even more "outside" view than Lindbeck's, and is thus properly suspect, hard as I have tried to view radical economics objectively. My comments rest largely on some of the major books and articles by New Left leaders, for example, *Monopoly Capital* by Paul Baran and Paul Sweezy (New York: Monthly Review Press, 1966) and Harry Magdoff's *The Age of Imperialism* (New York: Monthly Review Press, 1969); and a substantial sampling of the

A. Lindbeck limits his comments to the *economics* of the New Left. But the real flavor of the movement, it seems to me, goes far beyond economics. Theirs is a protest literature in the broadest sense of the term. Most of the writers (though not all) proclaim that modern American society is a mess, and modern America is a pretty awful place in which to live. It is a society of oppression and manipulation, basically oppression and manipulation of just about everybody by the greedy rich, and especially the giant corporations. The wrong moral values dominate our society. For example, Edwards, Reich, and Weisskopf's *The Capitalist System: A Radical Analysis of American Society* (the product of one of the major intellectual centers of radical economics, at Harvard) is organized around the question, "What's wrong in America?" Their answer is—"inequality, alienation, racism, sexism, irrationality, and imperialism." Certainly all of these alleged failings have something to do with economics, and economics can help understand them. But they go a long way beyond what most economists think of themselves as analyzing. Betty Friedan on women's alienation and Erich Fromm on the alienated consumer are examples of the readings included. The radicals argue that we economists view the world far too narrowly—our social welfare functions are all wrong. Perhaps they will become the complete social scientists to deal effectively with this list of problems, with the "correct" welfare functions. But as far as I can see, the evidence is yet to come—on that, and even on major contribu-

---

Review of Radical Political Economics and the *Monthly Review*, plus several of the new "readers" on radical economics, for example, David Mermelstein's *Economics: Mainstream Readings and Radical Critiques* (New York: Random House, 1970); Richard Edwards, Michael Reich, and Thomas Weisskopf's *The Capitalist System: A Radical Analysis of American Society* (Englewood Cliffs, N.J.: Prentice-Hall, 1971); and David Gordon's *Problems in Political Economy: An Urban Perspective* (Lexington, Mass.: D. C. Health and Co., 1970). This is obviously a very partial sample.

tions of radical economics to understanding the problems listed.

The literature of the New Left puts great stress on the "fundamental contradictions in capitalism." Unequal distribution of power, poverty, violence, alienation, and the like are cited. Maybe these are "fundamental contradictions in capitalism"; surely such tensions are deep and difficult in our society. But as I look around the modern world, I am struck by the fact that much the same problems seem to exist in noncapitalist societies to at least the same degree. Concentration of power, as best I read the evidence, is rather greater in most of the so-called noncapitalist countries than in nations like the United States, Canada, and those of Western Europe. Some of the most violent episodes in human history have occurred in noncapitalist nations—for example, the massive purges in both the USSR and Communist China during the past half century. Poverty, by any test I know, is a more serious problem in the noncapitalist world than in the so-called overdeveloped western capitalist nations.

Lindbeck, in the gentle way common to most Swedes, has suggested that the literature of the New Left is rather short on constructive suggestions on what we can do about the problems it so vividly stresses. Some of the problems are real ones, and only the foolish and the blind will disregard them. The New Left aids us by insisting on them. But I think an honest evaluation of radical analysis must put the criticism of lack of positive analysis and constructive prescription more strongly than Lindbeck does. Indeed, Professor Robert Solow, in a lively but serious recent debate with Professor John Gurley, defended the omission of radical economics from a recent overview volume on modern economics as follows: "In short, we neglected radical economics because it is negligible."[3] He was right. Solow takes the ac-

[3]*American Economic Review*, LXI (May 1971), 63.

cusations of Gurley that traditional economics fails to deal with the big issues, while radical economics does so, and dissects the radical claims to provide deeper understanding of the issues. Does the class and power struggle explain the income shares going to labor and property owners? Does "imperialism" explain the relative per capita income levels of different nations, developed and underdeveloped? Does concern for corporate profits explain the course of U.S. fiscal and monetary policy? Perhaps traditional economics leaves a lot unexplained, but Solow's attack surely leaves the radical analysis of the particular issues under debate looking like a king with few clothes. I commend both Gurley's thoughtful statement of what radical economics is all about and Solow's reply to all who are interested in the issue.

Paul Samuelson, in a deft introduction to Lindbeck's essay, reinforces Lindbeck's emphasis on the failure of the New Left to come to grips with the overriding question of how one *does* organize a society if we reject both the market and political bureaucracy. Try to explain how Skinner's Walden II utopia could long exist without monthly allowance checks from parents outside the community. Many of the New Left economists clearly know better, and it would be unfair to blame them for the naïveté of their fellows. But the main response of at least some New Left writers to such unpleasant questions is a kind of retreat into utopian primitivism. If only we were all men of goodwill and cooperated, the world would be good. This response is not untypical of youthful idealism over many generations. If only the world were so simple, and the problems were so easily solved!

B. Lindbeck has surprisingly little to say about the New Left's stress on imperialism, since imperialism is the foundation of capitalist growth, as the New Left sees it. Lindbeck is properly free to focus where he wishes, but the New Left without imperialism is a little like the play without Hamlet.

I have no space to deal with the issue in detail. Let me merely report two of my own reactions to the literature. First, I cannot find the data to support the great emphasis placed by the New Left on U.S. expansion in Southeast Asia, or indeed the other developing nations, as the foundation of U.S. domestic health and prosperity; the numbers just are not big enough, no matter what the chain of reasoning used. Second, even if profits of U.S. companies abroad are large (or in some sense "excessive"), it does not necessarily follow that the developing nations are worse off than they would have been without the U.S. investment. Voluntary exchange certainly does not guarantee equal benefits to both parties, but it presumably offers some benefit to each, or he would not participate in the deal, a fact unmentioned in much of the New Left rhetoric on imperialism.

C. As a graduate student at Chicago in the late 1930's, I was caught in the intellectual battle between Oscar Lange, Frank Knight, Henry Simons, and Jacob Viner on whether the socialist state did, in fact, present a preferable alternative to the market system in efficiently and equitably organizing the use of society's resources. They were exciting times, and the intellectual ferment was great. Did Lange's "On the Economic Theory of Socialism" effectively demolish the Hayek–Von Mises criticism that socialism could not work efficiently? Was the *Road to Serfdom* the road to understanding or wishful thinking? Did the Great Depression mark the collapse of capitalism predicted by Marx, or were the causes quite different? These were no mean intellectual issues, and first-rate minds were devoted to grappling with them.

Alas, I sense no comparable intellectual stimulus and tension in the literature of the New Left vis-à-vis conventional economics. The modern radical literature, like other literature, has its own "in" jargon. "Paradigms," "new perceptions of reality," and "new and higher levels of consciousness" are the new O.K. terms. The writers suggest that the New Left offers a new scientific paradigm (essentially a new framework, or way of thinking about the problems of the world) that enables us to see the world's problems as they really are. We are urged to lift our thinking to new and higher levels of consciousness—again, a new way of perceiving and understanding "reality." But saying that modern radical economics offers a new scientific paradigm does not make it so. Perhaps we need a new perception of reality to understand the world. But until the New Left shows us how their words give significant operational guidance, with some degree of scientific rigor, in analysis and prescription of the problems they cite, the rhetoric is often vivid, but not very helpful. I noted above, for example, the few attempts at serious follow-through on the sophisticated theoretical models of Kaldor and Joan Robinson, dealing with issues at the very core of the New Left attacks on modern capitalism and conventional economics.

But there are visible the beginnings of some serious scientific work, especially by some of the younger economists —attempts to provide careful empirical evidence on the propositions advanced by the New Left and comparisons between these propositions and those made by conventional economics. The Edwards-Reich-Weisskopf volume provides some examples. This way lies progress. To them I say, Right On!

It is striking that there is no real consensus among New Left writers, either economists or others, as to the basic documents on which the movement rests. My impression is that Baran and Sweezy's *Monopoly Capital* is the most widely cited major work, and indeed it represents a serious attempt to criticize the existing order and suggest positive alternatives to conventional economic analysis. But interestingly, the book seems to have little impact outside the ranks of the followers themselves. Indeed, J. K. Galbraith's *The New Industrial State* (hardly the work of a radical economist, given Galbraith's views plus his current establishment position at Harvard and as the elected reigning monarch of the entire economics profession for 1972) seems almost to have upstaged the Baran-Sweezy book. With a deft pen and just enough anti-establishment economic analysis to make life difficult for conventional economists, Galbraith has had a major impact on the thinking of both economists and the general public. Although the New Left economists hardly consider Galbraith one of their own, I suspect he may have done more to advance some of their points than all their works together.

D. The New Left has something important to say to us as teachers. Not, so far as I can see, that it actually offers a new scientific paradigm that opens up new avenues of understanding, or provides many new analytical concepts or constructive diagnoses and prescriptions. Nor does most of the literature have the vividness and "punch" I had expected. It is long on philosophical disquisitions on the nature of reality and levels of consciousness. There is much reference to Marxism, but little to the central analytical work of Marx in *Capital* and comparable writings. I suspect they like Engels rather better than Marx.

But the New Left prods conventional economics where it needs prodding. It demands that we face up to the tough problems of society and not merely to worrying about existence theorems and second-order conditions. It sweeps aside the spaghetti of elaborate curves in our diagrams, and asks, what about power and poverty? It asks the questions in undergraduates' minds—not the comfortable questions we can answer readily with our theoretical apparatus, but the tough questions that seem important to young people in the world around us. Until one has tried to explain to a group of radical undergraduates just what is the matter with the labor theory of value and just why most of the troubles of our society are not due to capitalists' greed and corporations' power, he has not really faced up to the problem of making economics meaningful to many young people today.

The New Left cares about young people; it *is* young people. It cares about undergraduates, and we might well learn from it. Paying more attention to students, and meeting their questions on their terms, not ours, is a sobering experience, but a very useful one. To be sure, the New Left overstates its criticisms of the conventional wisdom in economics. Comparison of the half dozen leading elementary textbooks today with those of the 1940's or the 1920's is a convincing answer to people who say that economics is increasingly "irrelevant"; the change is dramatic indeed. The traditional economics says that supply and demand analysis does work. Modern macroeconomics, even given its shortcomings, can tell us and our students more about containing inflation and unemployment than pages of New Left polemic about imperialism, power, and capitalist greed. But—the New Left has some good unanswered questions. It is up to both them and us to answer those questions, at both a research level and the undergraduate level that matters to our students. Dignified silence will get conventional economics few new followers—and indeed, we may learn some important things ourselves in trying to make answers convincing.

In conclusion, what of the New Left? From this outsider's inexpert view, it is an important challenge to conventional economics and to the modern mixed capitalist systems, representing a modern, mixed evolution from Marxism, Veblenism, and utopianism. (1) It challenges our (implicit or explicit) social welfare functions as improperly narrow and discipline-bound. (2) It (with the exception of some of the economists) insists that we substitute the New Left's own values in such welfare functions for those widely accepted in our (western capitalist) societies, and that we adopt revolutionary, if only vaguely specified, changes in the structure and operations of the existing economy. (3) It shows the beginnings of serious scientific research by some radical economists on the acceptability and practicality of its propositions compared to those of "traditional economics." I doubt that the New Left will fade away soon, nor should it. But a rising ratio of reason to rhetoric will make it a more productive challenge in the future.

COMMENT
Stephen Hymer and Frank Roosevelt
NEW SCHOOL FOR SOCIAL RESEARCH

INTRODUCTION

RADICALS USUALLY have trouble communicating with economists.[1] The reason is that the two are generally interested in different questions. At the moment, however, we are fortunate enough to have an economist who is interested in the same questions that activate radicals. For this reason, Assar Lindbeck's *The Political Economy of the New Left—An Outsider's View* is a useful book for presenting the radical critique of economics and setting the stage for further dialogue.

The questions being asked by the New Left are (1) what is the connection between corporate capitalism and the obvious evils in our society, and (2) how do we go beyond capitalism towards the achievement of a decent society? Lindbeck begins his book explicitly accepting the validity of these questions: "The salient features of New Left economics are ... its critique of present-day capitalist societies, with the important role played by large corporations, and the vision of how the economy should be reorganized" (p. 6).

The fact that Lindbeck begins with the right questions enables us to avoid sterile arguments about the internal consistency of his presentation and to concentrate instead on the general usefulness of economics in dealing with the questions we agree on. Along the way, however, we shall

Reprinted from *The Quarterly Journal of Economics*, November, 1972, pp. 644–57.
[1]In this discussion we follow Lindbeck's general practice of using the words "economic" and "economist" to refer to the *neoclassical* (or orthodox, traditional, conventional, bourgeois) type of economist-economic theory.

have to examine whether the method favored by Lindbeck does not in fact lead him to change the questions themselves—or dodge them altogether.

In evaluating the relationship between Lindbeck's economics and the questions raised by the New Left, we will use the now familiar notion of a "paradigm" developed by Thomas Kuhn.[2] A paradigm provides a fixed conceptual framework for scientific research, placing limits on the type of *questions* that can be asked, the *methods* that can be used, and the *answers* that are acceptable. Thus a paradigm is like a flashlight in that it allows the scientist to shed light on certain questions, while at the same time leaving large areas in the dark. It is our contention that Lindbeck, while pointing with one hand at the right questions, holds in his other hand a flashlight (the economics paradigm) that is shining in the wrong direction. Hence, he must either change the questions or point his flashlight in another direction (i.e., adopt a new paradigm). We shall find that insofar as he illuminates anything, he has changed the questions.

But the New Left will not tolerate changing the questions. For they have arrived at their questions not, as Lindbeck suggests most economists choose theirs, "by considerations of available analytical techniques" (p. 22), but through their experience. This experience began, as a rule, in the comfortable homes of the middle class. As Adam Smith noted, "Before we can feel much for others, we must in some measure be at ease ourselves."[3] Having been reared in conditions of of relative affluence and security, a new generation naturally became sympathetic to the plight of others subject to poverty, prejudice, and colonialism.

[2]*The Structure of Scientific Revolutions* (Chicago: University of Chicago Press, 1962).

[3]*The Theory of Moral Sentiments* (New York: Augustus M. Kelley, 1966), p. 297.

At first the new generation tried to overcome social injustice with the tools of its class: reason, technical knowledge, legal maneuvering, and electoral reform politics. They worked in settlement houses to assist poor people. They went to the South to help blacks obtain their civil rights. They peacefully protested the involvement of U.S. corporations in South Africa. They went abroad in the Peace Corps to aid people in the underdeveloped countries. They marched with Martin Luther King and against the war in Vietnam. They patiently tried to introduce reforms in the universities to make them responsive to students. And, finally, they publicized the shoddiness of consumer products and the destruction of the environment. But in all of these activities the newly aroused young people operated on the assumption that the various evils they fought were only imperfections in a basically sound system.

The results obtained by the young activists, however, did not measure up to their expectations. They discovered personally the violence backed up by law and government that was used against blacks; in underdeveloped countries they saw ruling elites cooperating with international business to obstruct the most obviously needed reforms; they saw that their university administrators would resist mild demands with incredible tenacity; they saw how social welfare programs and prisons terrorized and degraded the very people they were supposed to uplift; and, in politics young people found that even if they could rouse a large groundswell against the War and force a President to give up, it did not stop the War. From this experience, they began to wonder if there is not something fundamentally at fault in the system itself.

To the people who were now coming to see themselves as the New Left, the socioeconomic system appeared more and more clearly to be rotten at its roots. It tended both to encourage and to depend upon greed; it almost always placed a higher priority on things than on people; and its very foundations seemed to rest upon relations of domination and subordination. In 1933, Keynes had said of modern capitalism: "It is not intelligent, it is not beautiful, it is not just, it is not virtuous—and it doesn't deliver the goods."[4] The experience of the New Left had brought them to the point of agreeing with this opinion of Keynes.

The experience of the New Left also led them to Marx. Finding themselves unable to deal with the waste, injustice, alienation, and entrenched power in their society, these young people had arrived existentially at the point from which Marx began his critique of capitalism. They found that he offered an explanation of social problems that went deeper than any they had previously encountered. And they were attracted by his vision of socialism and communism.

But it was difficult for young people to gain access to Marx. His language seemed impenetrable, and there were hardly any courses in the universities to help people understand him. In fact, there were few who had any idea of what was different about Marx. When one of us was a graduate student in economics at MIT, he asked his professors if they knew of anything in Marx that might be valid but was not included in the economics curriculum. Most of them answered "nothing," but Paul Samuelson responded: "the class struggle."

In what follows, we will argue that it is essential to take into account the class struggle—i.e., the fact of antagonistic relationships between groups of people—if one wishes to understand what is going on in the world. With Marx, we see this struggle occurring in modern society mainly between workers and capitalists. And it is important to ob-

---

[4]"National Self-Sufficiency," *The Yale Review*, XXII (June 1933), pp. 755–769.

serve, again following Marx, that capitalists and workers confront each other in two separate but interconnected realms: (1) the sphere of circulation, and (2) the sphere of production. The sphere of circulation is the realm of the market where the various actors meet each other as owners of commodities intent on exchanging them. The sphere of production is the more important realm where we find not only the production of commodities going on but also the capital-labor relationship itself being reproduced.

We have introduced these distinctions at this point because they help to explain the differences between the economic and the Marxian paradigms. They also help, in our opinion, to account for the different degrees of usefulness of the two paradigms in providing answers to the questions raised by the New Left.

Until recently it did not seem that economists cared much one way or the other about the New Left. As Samuelson put it in his foreword to Lindbeck's book: "It says something for the complacency of American economics that, prior to Lindbeck's lecture (1969) at MIT, many of our graduate students had thought of the New Left as having something to do with politics, not with honest-to-goodness economics" (p. xii). But now Lindbeck has come over from Sweden to tell us that the New Left has something to say to economists and to claim that economists, in turn, have something to offer to the New Left: "When trying to evaluate the New Left criticism of economists, it is also important to note that considerable parts of economic analysis do in fact deal with exactly those problems in which the New Left seems to be interested," (p. 23). To evaluate this claim is one of the main purposes of the present essay. We will proceed first by reconstructing the economics paradigm from Lindbeck's discussion and then by comparing it to the Marxian paradigm. We will let the reader judge which paradigm comes closest to answering the questions of the New Left.

THE ECONOMICS PARADIGM

In his survey of the New Left's critique of economics, Lindbeck presents us with a balance sheet of the strengths and weaknesses of his way of looking at the world. First, he tells us what tools economics *has* for analyzing various social problems, and, a moment later, he is good enough to indicate what economics *lacks* (in several cases associating the name of Marx with the excluded concepts). We will find that the items on the negative side of Lindbeck's balance sheet add up precisely to the Marxian set of tools, and we will contend that these tools, when brought together, prove more useful in dealing with the problems Lindbeck is addressing. Let us now take the problems one by one, in the order established by Lindbeck, and set up the balance sheet.

1. *Distribution.* Lindbeck takes up the New Left's charge that "academic economists ... have insufficiently studied problems of the *distribution of income, wealth, and economic power* in society" (p. 9, itals in original). He concedes "that 'academic' economic theories of the distribution of income are still based on the marginal productivity analysis—and hence on demand-supply models ..." (p. 10) but dismisses the alternative theory of distribution that has recently been developed in Cambridge, England. Nowhere does he make clear that one of the chief differences between these two theories is that the first takes the existing distribution of wealth and economic power for granted (claiming that it will give the same results no matter who owns or controls what), while the second holds that nothing can be said until the general wage-profit division is determined (giving a central role to the distribution of wealth and economic power).

In contrast to the "academic" economists' theory of income distribution, Lindbeck correctly observes "that the emphasis in New Left writings is more on institutional arrangements and on the role of notions of the 'distribution of power' and the 'class struggle' in explaining the distribution of income" (p. 11).

2. *Tastes—Resource Allocation.* Here Lindbeck cites the New Left criticism "that economists tend to utilize too partial an approach in their analysis of . . . the problems of the *allocations of resources* . . . taking household preferences mainly as given, thereby leaving investigation of the formation of such preferences to other disciplines. . . ." Asserting that "today very little is known about the formation of preferences which is useful for economic analysis," Lindbeck concludes: "It does, therefore, seem that this criticism is well grounded . . ." (p. 12).

While Lindbeck clearly recognizes that preferences *change* (he calls for more studies of "the extremely complex mechanisms by which values and preferences are formed and changed"), he proceeds throughout the book to make policy recommendations—e.g., in favor of markets, reliance on material incentives—on the basis that they result in the optimal satisfaction of *given* consumer preferences. (See e.g., pp. 33, 34, 40, 71–72.) This procedure would be justifiable only if it could be assumed that the policies and institutions recommended have no effect on preferences. Since this is clearly not the case, Lindbeck's arguments—and indeed all normative conclusions drawn from the theory of "efficient" allocation of resources—are undermined.[5] It simply will not do to jump from ignorance of change to assumption of stasis.

At the root of the difficulty here is the "partial" approach of economics that takes preferences as being exogenously determined and then shifts the burden of studying their formation and change onto "other disciplines." The New Left rejects this compartmentalization and takes the Marxian

[5]Cf. Herbert Gintis, "Alienation and Power: Towards a Radical Welfare Economics," Ph.D. thesis, Harvard University, 1969.

view that preferences change endogenously—i.e., that new needs are created in the same process by which their means of satisfaction are produced.

3. *The Quality of Life.* Under this heading, Lindbeck brings up the New Left criticism that the quantitative orientation of economists leads them to "concentrate on the satisfaction of preferences for consumer goods, and possibly for leisure time, thus partly neglecting such problems as working conditions, the ways in which decisions are made, and the problem of the quality of the environment . . ." (p. 13). What strikes the critical reader of this section is that Lindbeck brings up *three* distinct problems (which in the next paragraph he refers to as: "Deterioration of the environment, alienation in work, and neglect of collective services") but only discusses *one* of them—the environment. This is no accident, for the only tool economists have to deal with "the quality of life" is the theory of "external effects."

Looking at qualitative problems in terms of "externalities" is a necessary consequence of the economists' focus on the sphere of circulation. If something is going wrong— e.g., poor working conditions, lousy decision making, fouled-up environment—it *must* be because people's preferences or firms' costs are not adequately represented in market prices. Hence the solution offered by the economists also falls in the realm of exchange: one must simply find out what the "external effects" are and induce people to take them into consideration by having the government tax or subsidize those market transactions that are causing all the trouble. (Cf. Lindbeck, pp. 14–15.)

Now this approach seems plausible when it is applied to environmental problems. (Companies might pump less waste into the river if they were taxed accordingly.) So this is the problem Lindbeck discusses. But what about "the ways in which decisions are made" and "alienation in work"? It is hard to see how any programs of taxes or subsidies might deal with these problems—even if we assume that such programs can actually be adopted and implemented by governments in capitalist societies. In fact one must leave the sphere of exchange and enter that of production even to understand these problems.

Lindbeck points in the right direction when he mentions —albeit condescendingly—what has been excluded from the economists' analysis, namely, "Marxist notions of the 'obsession' of capitalists with the accumulation of capital and the 'unlimited' expansion of production, regardless of other values in society" (p. 14). We contend that if one starts from these "notions" and keeps in mind the interest of capitalists in preserving the capital-labor relationship, it will be much easier to understand why "working conditions," "the ways in which decisions are made," and even "the quality of the general environment" have developed the way they have under capitalism.

4. *Large Versus Small Changes.* Here Lindbeck presents the New Left's charge that "economists are obsessed with *marginal changes* within a given economic system" and fail to "discuss large, *qualitative changes* in the economic system." There are really two issues here.

First, there is an issue that can be seen in terms of comparative statics. As Lindbeck puts it, "economists are criticized for confining their studies mainly to 'local optima,' in the neighborhood of the initial position, rather than asking whether there may be some superior 'total optimum' position in a society organized quite differently from those we know" (p. 16). This is the framework in which economists are relatively comfortable. While refraining from value judgments, they may speculate about "comparative economic systems." In this regard, Lindbeck applauds "the vast literature on market systems and the differences between central-ization and decentralization" but admits that "the literature on comparative economic systems is not among the strongest in economics" (p. 16).

The more serious omission on the part of economists is their neglect of the dynamics of historical change of eco-nomic systems. Here again, Lindbeck hints at the necessary but excluded analytical tools when he notes that "the crit-icism is given a Marxian touch by the New Left when they emphasize the need for the study of great historic processes and transformations of systems when their inherent 'contra-dictions' become too strong" (p. 16). That he himself has no use for such analysis is evident in his supercilious refer-ences to "the 'grand visions,'" found in much of the New Left literature, of the historical development of capitalist societies" (p. 1). What the economists are left with is a comparative blueprints approach that does not help them determine what policies are relevant to any particular his-torical situation.[6]

5. *The Role of Political Considerations.* We have now come full circle. Having begun by excluding "notions of the 'distribution of power' and the 'class struggle'" from his theory of how the economy works (marginal productivity analysis), Lindbeck finally returns to consider the New Left criticism of economists "for having neglected the *interaction between economic and political factors.* In particular, econ-

[6]The practical shortcomings of the economists' approach are re-flected in the sense of futility that pervades Lindbeck's description of his own proposal to reduce income inequality by expanding edu-cation: "However, then we are in the world of conventional liberal-social democratic policies, in which various kinds of inequalities in the distribution of income have always, though not necessarily suc-cessfully, been fought in this way (or at least it has been proposed to have them so fought)" (p. 58).

omists are said to have avoided problems of the distribution of power in the economy along with its implications for both domestic and foreign policies" (p. 17). But, of course! If economists consciously exclude power from their models, they will inevitably fail to understand what is going on in the world.

After a superficial discussion of the consequences of uneven distribution of power on both the domestic and international levels, Lindbeck concludes: "I think it is hard to deny that economists have had little to say about such problems, that is, about the relation between economic power and the political process" (p. 20). Later in the book, he himself serves as a good illustration of the economist's inability to say anything about questions involving power and the economy. Taking up the subject of imperialism again, he considers the view that the poverty of the under-developed countries "to a considerable extent is 'caused' by the affluence of rich countries and by the activities of cap-italist firms in underdeveloped countries." Given what Lind-beck himself has said previously about the competence of economists in these matters, we are hardly surprised that the economics paradigm allows him only to find this "a belief that is quite difficult to prove or disprove" (p. 32).

Let us now draw up Lindbeck's balance sheet for eco-nomics in a table. It is our contention that the items on the positive side of the balance sheet that form the basic tool kit of economics are insufficient for dealing with the New Left's questions. They relate exclusively to the sphere of circulation and thus cover only an arbitrarily circum-scribed area of economic phenomena. Within this frame-work the economist is constrained to move in one dimen-sion back and forth along a continuum with free markets at one end and central planning at the other.

QUESTION	INCLUDED IN ECONOMICS	EXCLUDED FROM ECONOMICS
Distribution	Marginal productivity theory	Distribution of power Class struggle
Tastes—allocation	Assumption of given preferences exogenously determined	Endogenous preference change Development of needs through productive activity
	Theory of efficient allocation of resources	
The quality of life: environment working conditions decision making	Theory of external effects	Drive to accumulate capital Capital-labor relationship
Large vs. small changes	Marginal analysis Comparative economic systems	Transformation of systems Contradictions (dialectical analysis)
Political considerations		Distribution of power and its role in the economy

But the capitalist process of production taken as a whole represents a synthesis of production and circulation. If we wish to understand the roots of the evils in our society and assess the posibilities of going beyond capitalism, we must be able to move also in the second dimension of production relations. This involves an analysis of the excluded items on Lindbeck's balance sheet, which, taken together, form the basis of the Marxian paradigm.

THE MARXIAN PARADIGM

The Marxian system begins with the process of production. In every mode of production, labor and means of production are united to produce output. But it is the specific manner in which this union is accomplished that distinguishes the different socioeconomic formations from one another. Under capitalism they are united through the wage-labor contract under which the laborer alienates his labor power and agrees to submit to the control of the capitalist or his representative during the process of production.

In the market the laborer was a "free agent" who owned his own labor power and dealt with the capitalist on equivalent footing in pursuit of his own private interest. The bargain completed, however, he finds himself no longer free or equal or a property owner or an individual but a subordinate in an authoritarian hierarchy working with and on materials he does not own in a collective process of production.

The dualism between freedom in the marketplace and authoritarianism in the workplace is the essential characteristic of capitalist society. If the marketplace furnishes the economist with the model to justify capitalism in terms of freedom, equality, possession, and individualism, the actual conditions of work furnish the New Left with the critique of capitalism (with its nonfreedom and nonequality) as well as the clues to a future society (with a nonpossessive and nonindividualistic organization of work).

When the worker sells his labor, he in effect surrenders his freedom; but this does not mean that he passively accepts capitalist production. The laborer's daily work is involuntary, and so each day involves a struggle between capital and laborer. The capitalist tries to get the worker to do something he or she does not want to do; the worker tries to resist doing it. In Volume I of *Capital*, Marx analyzes the capitalist system of production in terms of this constant struggle, showing the forms of resistance put up by the workers and the types of pressure (e.g., organization, introduction of machinery, social legislation) devised by the capitalist to maintain control over the workers' labor time. These problems, which lie outside the market sphere, are hardly touched on at all in the modern economics curriculum. Although detailed and explicit discussion of them can be found in the literature of corporate organization, personal relations, industrial sociology, and psychology, they are always approached from the point of view of control rather than resistance. One of the tasks of radical social scientists is to turn this literature on its head and develop counter-organization theories in continuation of Marx's work.

How does the market fit into this? In the market numerous buyers and sellers confront each other under more or less competitive conditions and exchange commodities according to the laws of supply and demand. This aspect has been extensively analyzed by economists. But they have neglected a second aspect: the constraints placed on the market outcomes by the need to maintain the capitalist nature of production. Volume II of *Capital* attempts to deal with this problem by showing how the circular flow of goods and money reproduces the capital-labor relation—i.e., results in a distribution of income and wealth such that the capitalists end up again owning the means of production and the laborers end up again having to sell their labor in order to live. The wage must be sufficiently high to maintain the laborer but not high enough to allow him to become a capitalist. For example, if wages rise and eat into profits, investment dries up, growth slows down and unemployment results. This exerts a downward pressure on wage demands, restores the rate of profit, and allows the capitalist system to go on.

When we examine the interconnections between markets and production, it becomes clear that we cannot restrict our methodology to the economic plane alone—consideration must be given to the political and ideological planes as well. It is only by breaking the ties that bind circulation and production together that economists can ignore the relations between economic and political power.

Since capitalism requires unequal relations of dominance and subordination in production, the game of the market must be a loaded game. The players begin with unequal endowments of wealth and education and at the end of play find themselves in much the same relative position as before. Of course a certain degree of mobility exists: a small number of people change ranks; but in cycle after cycle over the last two hundred years, the pyramid has remained a pyramid. In each round the top 10 percent of the population gets from 30 to 40 percent of the take, the bottom two thirds get only one third. The players are then ready to play again in production—the poor to work, the middle to manage, the rich to accumulate.

In one section of his book, Lindbeck abhors the existing distribution of income and wealth and proposes that it be made more equal. Here he is thinking at the level of the market: if we can somehow make the distribution of human capital more equal, people will be able to exchange their skills for relatively equal amounts of income. (Cf. Lindbeck, pp. 57–58.) However, in other places he favors maintaining wage differentials and relying on material incentives to get people to work. He can see wage differentials only "as incentives for efficiency, education, and training, or as a method of allocating labor to different jobs" (p. 69). We see them as necessary to the continuation of the capitalist mode of production.

Much force was needed to bring this system into being. Though economists have generally overlooked its brutal origins during the period of primitive accumulation in the sixteenth and seventeenth centuries, we can today see in the underdeveloped countries a replay of the violence of modernization. Pacification of the countryside, the police state, the pass system are the seeds and fertilization from which a free market is growing in the "backward" areas.

Once free markets are established, force takes on more respectable forms. One of these respectable forms is the education system where people are traind to accept competition, discipline, authoritarianism, rigid schedules in preparation for life in capitalist production. This form of coercive socialization has been of particular interest to the New Left and is being extensively investigated by radical economists using the tools of class analysis rather than the market methodology of human capital.[7]

Another respectable form of coercion is the propagation of ideologies that disguise the nature of human relations in our society. In our view, economics is one of the most important of these ideologies. By concentrating on market relations that mask the real nature of the transaction between capital and labor, economists have mystified the economic processes in our society and hindered the development of analytical tools for going beyond them.

While economists have focused on the relation between things—e.g., the price of apples in terms of bananas—Marx has pierced the veil of the market to discover its connection to the relations between people. Having started from an analysis of production in Volume I of *Capital* and traced through its connection of circulation in Volume II, he re-

[7]See Herbert Gintis, "Education, Technology, and the Characteristics of Worker Productivity," *American Economic Review, LXI*, No. 2 (May 1971), and "Towards a Political Economy of Education," *Harvard Educational Review*, LXII, No. 1 (Feb. 1972), 70–96. See also: Samuel Bowles, "Unequal Education and the Reproduction of the Social Division of Labor," *Review of Radical Political Economics*, III, No. 4 (Fall/Winter 1971), and "Contradictions in U.S. Higher Education," in Richard Edwards, Michael Reich and Thomas Weisskopf, eds., *The Capitalist System* (Englewood Cliffs, N.J.: Prentice-Hall, 1972).

turns in Volume III to the various forms capital assumes on the surface of society (in the actions of different capitals upon one another, in competition) and in the ordinary consciousness of the agents of production. In production, the capitalist is acutely conscious of the relation between himself and the laborer—but in circulation he is more concerned with his competitive relations with other capitalists. This concern leads to various illusions about the nature of the economy that serve in part to maintain the system by confusing the issues and in part to undermine the system by rendering it unable to handle continued economic progress. We cannot here describe these illusions in detail. We can only mention in passing the basic bias in the market relation in exaggerating the role of capitalist cunning and entrepreneurship and downgrading the importance of labor cooperation in advancing civilization. It is because of this set of blinders, according to Marx, that "The capitalist mode of production is generally, despite all its niggardliness, altogether too prodigal with its human material, just as, conversely, thanks to its method of distribution of products through commerce and manner of competition, it is very prodigal with its material means, and loses for society what it gains for the individual capitalist." [8]

CONCLUSION

In closing, let us return to consider the relevance of the two paradigms to the questions posed by the New Left. We remember that Lindbeck originally accepted the questions of the New Left and promised to show how economics can be applied to "its critique of present-day capitalist societies . . . and the vision of how the economy should be *reorganized*" (p. 6, italics added). By the end of the book,

Capital, Vol. III (New York: International Publishers, 1967), pp. 86–87.

however, he has indicated his acceptance of the "mixed economy"—i.e., the capitalist Welfare State—and argued that the only trouble with the United States is that it is underdeveloped! Thus, recalling our original metaphor, we find that the aim of Lindbeck's flashlight has induced him to change the questions.

As Lindbeck himself pointed out, the more you immerse yourself in the economics paradigm, the more conservative you become: "It is probably . . . true that many years of studying economics tend to increase respect for decentralization and markets" (p. 26). All problems become "market failures," and all solutions take the form of government intervention. But whatever is done, it must not interfere with the making of profits: "As economists have long tired to show, it is very difficult to find a better *criterion* for efficiency in the allocation of resources, in accordance with given consumer preferences, than that of production being directed according to profit prospects . . ." (pp. 70–71).

The Marxian paradigm offers an alternative perspective and produces a different set of answers. It shows that capitalism, because it is based on private property and promotes an individualist point of view, places strict limits on how much government interference it will tolerate. It argues that as the system advances, the contradiction between its social nature and its private organization becomes increasingly intense. And it recommends that we supersede the mode of production based on wage labor by striving consciously to control our own everyday life in production as well as in consumption.

The growing emphasis on econometrics should make economists increasingly aware of the biases and incorrect policy proposals that result from models that exclude important variables and equations. We have tried to show in this article that the balance sheet drawn up by Lindbeck accurately represents the serious misspecification problem of the economics paradigm. We hope that Lindbeck's book stimulates a fruitful dialogue between radical and traditional economists on how to go beyond our present limitations in thought and action.

COMMENT
Paul M. Sweezy

THE MONTHLY REVIEW

THE NEW LEFT—OLD LEFT dichotomy from which Lindbeck starts seems to me more misleading than helpful, and in fact he is able to maintain it only by a strategem of dubius validity. He prudently refrains from attempting to provide a definition of either kind of Left, but in order to write about the New Left he is obliged to select certain writers as spokesmen, or as he says in one place (p. 53), "inspirers" of the movement whose views can be cited and criticized. Who are they? Thumbing back through the text and footnotes, I find the following names, most of them occurring more than once and some rather frequently: Herbert Marcuse, Harry Magdoff, André Gunder Frank, Ernest Mandel, Baran and Sweezy (separately and in combination), André Gorz, Leo Huberman, and (with reservations and qualifications) John Kenneth Galbraith.

Now, whatever else these people may or may not be, they are certainly not in any sense "new." Quite a few have been identified with the Left for thirty-five years or more, and every one of them had a pretty well-defined political identity long before there was anything called the New Left. How does it happen that they now appear as ideologists of a movement that probably everyone would agree dates from the second half of the 1960's? This is a question that Lindbeck never raises, quite possibly because it never occurred to him. And yet the answer is neither obscure nor unimportant to an assessment of his critique.

Reprinted from *The Quarterly Journal of Economics*, November, 1972, pp. 658–64. Copyright © October 1972 by Monthly Review, Inc. Reprinted by permission of Monthly Review Press.

What these writers—apart from Galbraith, of course, who is a special case and is treated as such by Lindbeck too—and at least parts of the New Left have in common is a total rejection of the whole capitalist-imperialist system and a profound lack of interest in schemes or efforts to reform it (except as they may be related to revolutionary tactics). They both also see the Soviet Union and its Eastern European satellites as class societies increasingly indistinguishable from their capitalist counterparts and hence capable of teaching only negative lessons. On many other matters —theoretical analysis, strategy and tactics, the nature of a good society—these writers differ greatly among themselves, as indeed do the New Leftists. Nevertheless, the points of convergence are undoubtedly important and provide a plausible basis for treating this particular group of "old" Leftists as spokesmen for the New Left. Only it should be clear that what is involved here is not really an old-new dichotomy but rather a radical-reformist dichotomy, which is certainly as old as the modern socialist movement and which exists in every generation. It comes to the fore now because the generation of Leftists that emerged on the scene in the late 1960's was heavily weighted on the radical side.

Up to this point I have provided a sort of rationale for Lindbeck's methodology. Let me hasten to add, however, that this is all very unfortunate for Lindbeck because, while he is committed to discussing the radical position, he is singularly ill equipped to do so. He has no empathy for the radical position; his view of history and the historic process is totally different; and his understanding of Marxism, the only coherent intellectual tradition to which the radical Left can relate, is exactly what one would expect of a very conventional neoclassical economist, i.e., superficial to the point of nonexistence. The result is that while to Paul Samuelson (see his Foreword) and perhaps to most of the rest of Lindbeck's professional colleagues the book is fresh and stimulating, I, as a radical, find it as irrelevant and boring as most neoclassical economics.

The biggest difference between Lindbeck and us is that we see two totally different realities. He has the typical liberal-reformist view of history as essentially a series of accidents: nothing had to happen the way it did, and from now on anything can happen. The future is therefore a kind of smorgåsbord offering all the dishes in the liberal cookbook from which "we" can choose those that most appeal to us. War and violence and revolution are very costly in human lives and suffering, so "we" naturally reject them. It is better to take what there is, imperfect though it may be, and fix it up in accordance with the tried and true principles of consumer sovereignty, competition (*any* kind of competition will do, see p. 79), profit maximization, etc., etc., interfering here and there to get some of the things that this system does not provide, like more equality and more public goods and services. As far as the relations between developed and underdeveloped countries are concerned, the problem is not exploitation or anything like that but rather a natural tendency of the big and the strong to dominate the small and the weak. Here, as at various other points of his argument, Lindbeck brings in the Soviet Union, which, since it also qualifies as an imperialist country, "proves" that imperialism has nothing to do with capitalism or socialism. (He might at least have the grace to say, maybe in a footnote, that so far, at any rate, the Soviet Union has refrained from dropping napalm on backward countries halfway around the world out of "long-term considerations of national security," which he considers to be "maybe the crucial consideration" determining the foreign policy of the big powers [p. 63].)

The radical view of the world is of course entirely different. We see the present as the frightful outcome of some four centuries of the history of capitalism, a system the very heart of which is exploitation and inequality and which is now careening out of control toward its final crises and catastrophes. Wars and revolutions are not a matter of preference or choice: they are the inevitable outcome of capitalism's inner contradictions, and the question is not whether they will happen but whether they will finally do away with the system that breeds them. To speak of reforming capitalism is either naïveté or deception. Wealth, privilege, and power go together and belong to a class that will fight to the end to preserve its monopoly over them, allowing only such reforms and freedom to reformers as it deems to be in its own interest. As for the Soviet Union, it is the product of a genuine anticapitalist revolution but one which, for reasons that are only beginning to be properly understood, was unable to carry through to a nonexploitative, classless society. It is therefore, once again, naïveté or deception to cite the Soviet Union to prove anything about socialism: it is not a socialist society and, even more important, it is not moving toward socialism but away from it. (I might add, speaking for myself and what I believe is a growing proportion of the radical Left, that the lessons of Soviet experience have not been lost on the world revolutionary movement and that partly as a result of these lessons, China has been able to move, not without setbacks and retreats, toward socialism and has already created a society radically different from capitalism.)

I do not of course expect Lindbeck to accept or even understand this radical view of reality. From his standpoint it is probably either ridiculous or nonsensical, and nothing I can say is likely to induce him to change his mind. If this is so, however, the question inevitably arises as to what value or importance Lindbeck can possibly have as a critic of the radical Left. And the answer is the obvious one: very little if any.

There is another way of looking at Lindbeck's book, i.e., as the informal commentary of a more or less typical neo-classical economist on a wide range of problems that he thinks are important. (From this point of view, the fact that he thinks the radical Left must also think them important and hence must entertain views about them that can reasonably be compared with his own can be ignored.) In other words, Lindbeck's book could easily provide a convenient starting point for a critique not of the radical Left but of neoclassical economics. I do not aspire to anything so ambitious and will therefore confine the remainder of these remarks to a couple of topics on which lack of clarity seems particularly prevalent.

There is first the whole question of the formation and role of consumer preferences. For a long time the standard, if seldom articulated, view of bourgeois economics was that the wants and preferences of consumers are an emanation of human nature, rising in an endless ladder from the simplest requirements for food, clothing, and shelter to the demands of the educated sensibility for all the refinements and luxuries of advanced civilization. At every income level needs and wants are identical and universally shared. It follows automatically that, apart from the distribution of income, about which legitimate differences of opinion may exist, and apart from the provision of goods and services that can only be consumed collectively, it is absolutely impossible to make out a rational case against allowing consumer preferences to play the dominant role in determining the allocation of resources and the composition of social output. Precisely when this view was first challenged I do not know, but it certainly came under what may be called preliminary questioning as early as Pigou's pioneering work in welfare economics; and in recent years it has been subjected to concerted attack from several quarters (latter-day muckrakers like Vance Packard, Galbraith, etc.). The argument of these bourgeois iconoclasts of course is that consumer preferences are manipulated by monopolistic advertisers and salesmen and that wants therefore no longer reflect true needs, and the whole rationale of "consumer sovereignty" is therefore exploded.

The orthodox response to this line of argument has usually been to admit that there is some truth to it but not enough to invalidate the underlying case for respecting consumer preferences. It is true that people do not need chrome-covered cars with new models every year, but they do need cars; and, as failure of the Edsel and the growing popularity of imported economy cars show, there are limits to their manipulatibility. Excesses thus tend to produce their own correctives, and the total social costs involved are not all that great anyway.

If the debate is confined to this level, it seems to me that the orthodox clearly have the better of it. But from the radical point of view these arguments and counterarguments do not even scratch the surface of the problem. What is this need for cars?[1] It is real enough, no doubt about that. According to a Gallup survey, 81 percent of American workers travel to and from work by automobile (*New York Times,* May 30, 1971). Most of them could not get there any other way, so their need for cars is as real as their need for jobs. But is this a need that emanates from human nature, or is it a need that has been created by a certain

[1] I take the case of cars because it is a particularly striking one, but the analysis applies, *mutatis mutandis,* to the whole range of wants and needs.

kind of society? The answer of course is obvious. It follows that the question to ask about cars is not whether the consumer is manipulated into buying one kind or another, but whether a society that makes it necessary to have a car in order to get to work makes any sense. Note that what is at issue here is not only the mode of transportation but, even more important, a locational pattern that implies the universal separation of residence and work. Not only is this pattern of separation a very recent phenomenon historically, but also it exists in this extreme form only in the United States. (The Gallup survey referred to above found that in West Germany, the second most car-using country of seven investigated, only 45 percent of workers travel by car, while 22 percent, as compared to only 6 percent in the United States, walk to work.)

Presented with information of this kind, an orthodox neoclassical economist could be expected to react in several ways. In the first place, he will probably see car use as an index of "modernization," definitely a good thing in his book. That the United States is ahead of the others demonstrates that it is the most modern and shows them the shape of their own future. If you suggest to him that some countries may not want to follow this course, he will disagree with you and point to the Soviet Union and Eastern Europe as proof that the desire to possess automobiles is so strong that no government can long resist it. It is not that this desire emanates from human nature, he will explain in anticipation of a possible objection, but simply that the technology of automotive transport exists and people will insist on benefiting from it. (At bottom your neoclassical economist is very much a technological determinist, though he is so little aware of it that he is given to (wrongly) condemning Marxism for allegedly subscribing to a doctrine of technological determinism.) If you point out that the "benefits" of automobilization on the U.S. scale include such things as urban decay and breakdown, growing and perhaps irreversible destruction of land and pollution of air, and much else that most reasonable people do not consider particularly beneficial, he will probably launch into a discussion of externalities and how to deal with them through taxation and subsidies (in this case he might suggest taxation of urban car use and subsidization of public transportation). If you express skepticism on the ground, among others, that the automobile-industrial complex seems to have an awful lot of power, he will admit that you have a point but will quickly dismiss it with the admonition that the real trouble is not so much the power of special interests as the apathy of the public. And if you finally explode with some such statement as that the whole rotten system is nothing but an externality of profit making and capital accumulating, he will be confirmed in his original suspicion that you are a nut who is incapable of understanding the objective and value-free science of economics. You will not, alas, have reached a meeting of the minds, but at least you will have temporarily succeeded in lifting the discussion of the needs, wants, and preferences of consumers above the level of banalities and trivialities on which it usually moves.

A final matter on which I would like to comment is the neoclassical economist's worship of innovation. Lindbeck reflects this attitude in a number of passages, but nowhere more explicitly than in connection with what he calls "market socialism":

A . . . *specific* problem for socialist market economies seems to be designing ways for individuals to take *new* initiatives (such as the development of new products, new firms, and new production techniques) when private ownership in the sphere of production is not permitted.

If only those who have succeeded in reaching the top levels of the prevailing hierarchies are allowed to take initiative, it is not likely that initiative will be hampered? . . . It is not obvious that such problems can be avoided in a less hierarchical system of organizations *within* firms (for instance, with voting rights and majority decision-making for all employees). In this case too, it may be difficult to launch new ventures if on every occasion the majority has to be convinced that a new product is worth producing and a new method of production worth applying. Another complication is the difficulty of convincing the majority in a firm that a plant should be moved to another region or possibly be closed down completely (pp. 67–68).

Quite apart from arguments about whether this or that arrangement is conducive to various forms of innovation in products and methods of production, what is conspicuously absent here, and throughout neoclassical economics, is any reasoned support for the view that innovation in these areas is a highly desirable characteristic of any economic system. This is simply taken for granted as self-evident. To me, and I would suppose to many others not already bemused by the tenets of economic orthodoxy, it is anything but self-evident. Why would it not be preferable to develop good products (functional, aesthetically attractive, durable) and methods of production compatible with humanized labor processes and then stick to them until or unless some rational reason for change is persuasively offered? In other words, why not a presumption *against* rather than *for* innovation as such? As for Lindbeck's "difficulty of convincing the majority in a firm that a plant should be moved to another region or possibly be closed down altogether," I would ask, why assume that production must always be organized in firms or plants that can be moved or closed down? Why not in communes that are social and political as well as economic units, that are located in a certain place because they are part of the whole lives of their members, and that it would never occur to anyone to close down? I think I know the answer to these questions. It is that innovation is good for the capitalist economy: it creates obsolescence, or stimulates new demand, or opens additional outlets for capital investment, all of which tend to sustain effective demand and profits. And of course capitalist enterprises have to be organized in such a way that they can be moved or closed down in case they incur losses, or more profitable opportunities are available elsewhere. The same considerations hold for market "socialism," which in reality is only a somewhat different form of capitalism. Moreover, it is only natural that neoclassical economists should work on the principle that "what is good for capitalism is good." I only wish that they could achieve a degree of self-understanding sufficient to admit that this *is* their principle and to proclaim it as openly as we radicals proclaim the opposite.

HOW TO IDENTIFY NEW LEFT ECONOMICS?

A FIRST OBVIOUS DIFFICULTY in discussing the economic ideas of the New Left, is, of course, how to identify New Left economics. The solution that my book, *The Political Economy of the New Left*, attempts to provide for this problem is perhaps best described by indicating the general background to my study.

I started by collecting and reading radical political literature circulating at some U.S. campuses (mainly Columbia and Berkeley) during my stay in the United States in 1968–1969. The next step was to go to the articles, periodicals, and books that were quoted in, or seemed to have inspired, the radical campus literature. The track immediately led to contemporary Marxists and revolutionary socialists of an older generation, such as Baran, Sweezy, Mandel, Bettelheim, Gorz, Huberman, Magdoff, Frank—as well as to classical communists such as Marx, Lenin, Trotsky, and Gramsci. As both ideas and formulations in the New Left campus literature obviously were borrowed from, or at least invoked by, this older generation of Marxists and revolutionary socialists, I decided to pick references and quotations from these inspirers of the radical campus literature, rather than to quote the still rather unknown students and journalists who are writing it. Samples from radical campus literature in other countries in the West suggest that this traces back to about the same authors as the "corresponding" U.S. literature.

Paul Sweezy seems to agree with my procedure for identifying New Left ideas when he says that "the points of

Reprinted from *The Quarterly Journal of Economics*, November, 1972, pp. 665–683.

convergence are undoubtedly important and provide a plausible basis for treating this particular group of 'old' leftists as spokesmen for the New Left." Evidently Hymer-Roosevelt too accept my specification of New Left ideas. However, Sweezy also argues—as a criticism of my book—that "what is involved here is not really an old/new left dichotomy but rather a radical/reformist dichotomy." I agree, of course, that the radical-reformist controversy is basic to an understanding of the New Left discussion, and in fact my book consists, to a large extent, of a comparison of the radical (revolutionary) and reformist approach to economic and social change. However, I think Sweezy makes a mistake when he minimizes the usefulness of making a new-old left dichotomy also: the usefulness of a distinction between radicals and reformists does not necessarily make a distinction between old and new leftists irrelevant. For there are specific features in much of the New Left literature which make it differ from many earlier revolutionary writings. First of all, there is a different *emphasis* in much of the New Left literature, as compared to the bulk of the old left writings. Second, there are some *new* ideas in New Left writings that were not typical of most old left writings.

For instance, there is much more emphasis in the New Left literature on the concept of alienation—an idea particularly characteristic of the young Marx and his Hegelian predecessors. And the concept of class struggle is broadened in New Left writings to refer to a *general* competition for power among various groups in a complex social structure —a competition in which the struggle about the distribution of income (the surplus value) is only one aspect among several.[1] Other typical emphases in New Left literature, as

---

[1]Moreover, the Baran-Sweezy "surplus" is a very different animal from the original Marxists' "surplus value." See my book, *The Political Economy of the New Left* (New York: Harper & Row, 1971), pp. 73–74.

compared to many old left writers (for instance, Lenin), are the rather strong preference expressed for decentralization, and the vision of a society built on producers' cooperatives with a nonhierarchical and nonbureaucratic decision-making structure—ideas reminiscent of pre-Marxist socialists such as Fourrier, Proudhon, and Owen. On the basis of such preferences, it is easy to understand that the New Left, unlike the old left, is highly critical of the Soviet Union. In fact, one (somewhat oversimplified) way of defining the difference between the old and the New Left is to compare their different attitudes towards the Soviet Union. (However, many of the inspirers of the New Left were strong adherents of the Soviet Union, as well as of Joseph Stalin, before Khrushchev's de-Stalinization speech in 1956 and the subsequent attempt at counterrevolution in Hungary.)

Another specific feature of the New Left is the degree to which they have been influenced by recent non-Marxian critiques of the modern "corporate society," such as Herbert Marcuse, C. Wright Mills, and John Kenneth Galbraith. Examples are the ideas of the manipulation and the artificial nature of consumer preferences; the emphasis on externalities and the "quality of life"; the idea of an emerging symbiosis between private firms and the modern capitalist state (an idea found also in some old left writings, about "the last stage of capitalism"); the emphasis on the increased importance of intellectuals in the production process as well as on their roles as social reformers or revolutionaries; the idea that the educational system is largely subordinate to the interests of the central public administration and the large corporations. There are also some features of *part* of the New Left that presumably are connected with the emergence of an affluent, highly organized society in the West. This is reflected both in concern about "overconsumption," and a critique of Big Government and Big Labor as well as of Big Business.

Many of these new features are probably connected with the fact that the New Left is a students' movement rather than a workers' movement. Thus its adherents have usually not had experience in the labor market or with the practical problems of supporting and raising a family. (In fact, Hymer-Roosevelt give an illuminating historical sketch of how a group of idealistic university students with affluent family backgrounds wound up in a revolutionary New Left position, after being frustrated in their overoptimistic attempts to change society rapidly in line with their own preferences through the ordinary democratic procedures.)

On the basis of observations of this type—other illustrations could be provided—I still think it is useful to make a distinction not only between revolutionaries and reformists but also between the old and the New Left. The New Left ideas cover a *subset* of the old left ideas plus a *subset* of ideas developed by modern non-Marxian critics of bureaucratic societies, including both the USSR and the modern corporate society. The important thing, however, is not what we decided to *label* certain ideas. It is enough that we agree *what* ideas we are talking about; and on the latter point Sweezy, as well as Hymer-Roosevelt, seems basically to agree with me.

ARE THE WEAKNESSES OF TRADITIONAL ECONOMICS THE STRENGTH OF MARXISM?

A main point in the Sweezy paper, as well as in Hymer-Roosevelt's, is that academic economists and New Leftists are interested in completely different questions. There is some truth in this statement. One of the main points in my book was to show that we *should* be interested in the same questions. There are at least two reasons for this: (1) we are all living in the same world; and (2) every economic system has to solve very much the same problems.

What I tried to illustrate in my book was *both* that academic economists have dealt too little with a number of important economic and social problems in which New Leftists and Marxists are particularly interested, *and* that much of traditional economic theory nevertheless is quite relevant for many problems about which the New Left is or ought to be concerned.

Hymer-Roosevelt try to defend their lack of interest in and appreciation for traditional economics by talking about the existence of different "paradigms." Traditional economic theory is said to be a "flashlight" (or "paradigm") "which is shining in the wrong direction." Sweezy goes even further when he says that traditional economists and radical economists "see two totally different realities," which difference is said to make my book "as irrelevant and boring as most neoclassical economics" is to radical (revolutionary) economists. Sweezy tries, in fact, to make his ideas invulnerable to criticism from outsiders, when he implies that Marxism cannot be understood by those who lack "empathy for the radical position." It would seem that Sweezy is quite close to the opinion that Marxism is so delicate that it is impossible for those who do not *believe* in it to understand it.

I cannot accept this position, which is basically antiintellectual. If the impossibility of intellectual communication between different groups of social scientists is accepted, these groups belong in (different) divinity schools rather than in social science faculties of universities. Let us, then, look for a moment at the problems dealt with, and those not dealt with, by traditional economists and new leftists. As Hymer-Roosevelt point out, I have tried in my book to discuss a number of subjects that are not very well analyzed by academic economists: (1) the *dynamic* aspects of the distribution of income and wealth, in particular their development over time, and their relation to the whole legal, social, and cultural structure of a society; (2) the formation of preferences; (3) the quality of life, such as externalities, working conditions, and the ways decisions are made; (4) big *qualitative* changes in economic and social systems; and (5) the interaction between economic and political factors. It would seem that New Left criticism of traditional economists focuses mainly on these fields.

It is quite possible that the academic tradition in economics—following, in part, conventions about the borders of economic analysis established by the neoclassical pioneers —is partly responsible for the relative neglect of several of these important problems. However, there may very well be another reason for the underdeveloped state of scientific methods and knowledge in several of these fields: they may be particularly difficult to handle. For instance, the rather well-developed technique of marginal analysis is not sufficient and the problems are typically interdisciplinary in character, which creates special difficulties.

It would seem that both Sweezy and Hymer-Roosevelt, on the basis of the rather reasonable assertion that traditional economic theory has not been particularly successful in dealing with several of these problems, draw two main conclusions: that economic theory has practically *nothing* of interest to tell about them; and that Marxism, or New Leftism, has *much* to teach us about these very problems. Are these conclusions well founded?

It is quite possible, of course, that some tools and insights developed by Marx and his successors have a bearing on some of these problems. For instance, the Marxian emphasis on the *interrelations* between technology, the forms of economic and social organization, and politics is certainly helpful in analyzing long-term changes in social, economic, and political systems. In fact, this emphasis is shared by many non-Marxian scholars. To explain transformations of societies over time by the inconsistencies between different structures in a society, and by the competition between classes, certainly may be of great interest also. Thus, Marxian theory has undoubtedly supplied some interesting, though *partial*, hypotheses about long-term historical processes—a problem dealt with only slightly by most neoclassical economists, though certainly by a number of other non-Marxian social scientists, from Adam Smith, David Ricardo, Thomas Malthus, and John Stuart Mill to Max Weber, Joseph Schumpeter, Friedrich Hayek, Arnold Toynbee, and a number of contemporary historians and sociologists. I think the Marxists should admit more readily that their approach to the philosophy of long-term historical processes is only one among many, and that it is very difficult to discriminate among different hypotheses in this very field.

Moreover, if we look at the five "neglected" subjects in economics mentioned above, it would seem to me that many achievements in recent years in these fields have been made by economists with a rather traditional kit of tools. Some examples of such contributions are analyses of the determinants of the distribution of income and wealth and its change over time, using the theory of investment in human capital and allowing for such factors as family background, education, and training; the economics of information and learning-by-doing; the development over time of consumption patterns, including changes in preferences; studies of poverty, discrimination, and urban decay, and the analysis of externalities and their bearing on the "quality of life"; the implications of centralization and decentralization in economic systems and studies of "the politics" of economic policy (the relation between economic and political factors); and empirical studies of the economic relations between rich and poor countries, for instance with respect to capital movements and trade, etc.

There is certainly a long way to go before we can say that

we understand these problems very well. But on what
grounds do Marxists and New Leftists claim that *they* have
the answer to, or a better understanding of, these difficult
and important problems? Do Marxist economists have
better explanations, for instance, of why the share of labor
income has been rising during the postwar period in many
highly developed capitalist countries; and why wage differentials between industries have tended to rise in some countries (such as the United States), while they have tended to
be constant in other countries (such as Sweden); and why
certain minority groups are discriminated against in some
countries but privileged in other countries? Or are Marxists
able to give a more powerful explanation for the deterioration of the environment, and to show methods to improve
it, than are provided by the theory of externalities? Or have
the Marxists solved, or even dealt with, the problems about
the optimum mix of centralization and decentralization in
economic systems? Have the Marxists developed models,
other than market systems, to avoid centralization, bureaucratization, and an enormous concentration of power in the
context of highly developed societies? And can they explain
why and how consumption patterns have changed just the
way they have—in the United States and the USSR (without
relying at least partly on neoclassical tools such as income
and price elasticities and theories of learning processes)?
And, in the field of interaction between political and economic factors on an international level, for instance imperialism, have Marxists really given convincing, specific, and
empirically based explanations for the U.S. presence in
Vietnam and the Soviet presence in Eastern Europe? (I
accept Bach's critique that I have paid too little attention
in my book to the problems of imperialism and colonialism.
It is mainly my awareness of ignorance which has held me
back on these issues.) Or has the New Left given us particu-

larly good explanations of the conflict between the Soviet Union and China? The list of questions can be extended ad infinitum.

So far as I can see, Marxian economists have at most made *general statements* about some *concepts* that are *asserted* to be both useful and necessary for explanations about these phenomena. If Marxian economists really have *specific and empirically founded* answers to questions of this type, why do they not present them, if possible in forms susceptible to empirical tests? Before it has been demonstrated that Marxian theory gives particularly powerful explanations for these problems, it seems rather pretentious to assert that Marxian theory has the answers.

General talk about class struggle, distribution of power, development of needs through production activity, a drive for capitalists to accumulate, capital–labor relations, contradictions, and dialectics is surely not enough, until these concepts have been made concrete and used to explain *specific* empirically observable phenomena. Until some indication has been given of the power of Marxian theory to explain these specific issues, or similar ones, I think it is necessary to assume that we are all rather ignorant about many aspects of these difficult problems.

Thus, when Hymer-Roosevelt present a table of problems on which traditional theory is particularly silent—a list in fact derived from my study—this is hardly evidence that Marxian concepts will open the doors for an understanding of these topics. The fact that traditional theory has important lacunae hardly proves that *Marxism* (or Hinduism, fascism, mysticism, "Toynbeeism") is necessary to understand these issues. Just to present a column vector of general Marxist *terms* is certainly not enough.

These reflections are, of course, no denial of the fact that a number of young economists calling themselves "radical economists" or "revolutionaries," are making or will make important contributions to economic research, including empirical studies. However, much of the methodology of this research has, as Bach points out, a rather conventional flavor. In fact, it is often difficult to see what is radical, Marxist, or revolutionary in this research—except possibly some tendencies in the choice of topic, some emphasis on competition among socioeconomic power groups, and sometimes an inclination to add personal, subjective value terms (occasionally borrowed from Marxist jargon) to the analysis.

It may be of interest to look a little more closely at two *specific* analytical problems that both Sweezy and Hymer-Roosevelt seem to regard as particularly important: the formation of preferences and the distribution of power.

THE FORMATION OF PREFERENCES

It is quite simple, although it may seem "profound," to argue that traditional economists only deal with surface problems when they study and design mechanisms, such as a market system, to direct production in accordance with *existing* preferences—preferences that may be influenced by the production process itself. Is it not much more beautiful to promise, like the radical left, to create a system where production will be directed according to the "true," unmanipulated "needs" of consumers and voters?

The problem of preference formation and the value of respecting existing preferences is of course an old philosophical issue. However, there are a number of obvious questions that should be asked of people who believe that they know the true needs of individuals, or that they know how to find out these true needs. First of all, *who* should decide what are the true needs, or the preferences worth respecting? Second, what is wrong with the ambition to satisfy preferences that are the result of the production process itself? For instance, practically all cultural and artistic products—from Beethoven to the Beatles—obviously are examples of products for which demand is "created" by their supply. Would people become more happy if we created a system where producers, for ordinary consumers' goods as well as art, were not *allowed* to influence peoples' preferences, without first asking some political decision makers, or a system where *existing* preferences were not respected?

Would not, in fact, the refusal of politicians and administrators in a society to respect *existing* consumer preferences result in a rather authoritarian society, where the leaders decide what goods people should consume? In fact, the argument that existing consumer preferences are not worth respecting is a very close parallel to the classical totalitarian view—fascist as well as communist—that people do not understand their own interest, as under "other" circumstances they would wish to get not what they now demand, but what a leading elite benevolently wants to give them.

It is, of course, on the basis of considerations of this type that traditional liberal economists have found it of much value to design methods for respecting *existing* consumer preferences. It is for the same reason that adherents of political democracy have found it worthwhile to design methods—general elections—for respecting *existing* political preferences, in spite of the fact that these preferences also are not an "emanation of human nature" (quote from Sweezy) but are, rather, influenced by the historical development and present structure of the entire society, including propaganda (advertisement) by political parties and pressure groups (including the old and new left).

The reason why many people believe it worthwhile, and

even important, to accept existing preferences, with regard to both products and political parties, is of course *not* that preferences are assumed to be exogenous (an "emanation of human nature") but that this respect for individual choice *reduces the risk of the emergence of a totalitarian society.*

This pragmatic approach to the issue does not, of course, solve any philosophical problems about the nature of preferences, or about what we "really" do when satisfying preferences, which themselves are influenced by the whole structure of society. However, I believe it offers an argument for respecting existing preferences that many people can accpt.

Moreover, the fact that we are all influenced by the historical development and present state of society does not *logically* imply that individuals should be denied the right to satisfy what *they believe* are their wants and preferences ("existing preferences"). It is therefore quite beside the point when Hymer-Roosevelt, following Marcuse and Galbraith, argue that since "it cannot be assumed that the policies and institutions recommended have no effect on preferences," the argument that existing preferences should be respected—"and indeed all normative conclusions drawn from the theory of 'efficient' allocation of resources—are undermined."

The issue about the value of respecting *existing* preferences is not a question of "logic." It is a question of the choice between a rather decentralized, pluralistic society and a centralized, and therefore also more authoritarian, society.

It also follows that there is no logical contradiction between a desire to satisfy *existing* preferences and *a desire to change* the structure of society, thereby influencing preferences (often in a rather unknown way). It is quite true, as Sweezy points out, that, for instance, preferences for cars are likely to be influenced by the ways cities are built, by the geographical distribution of employment and housing, and by the organization of collective transportation. It is also quite obvious that we can hardly avoid considering how preferences are influenced when decisions in city planning are made. However, there is no *logical* difficulty in arguing that it is worthwhile to respect the preferences for cars that actually exist (for instance, to prevent the frustration of unsatisfied demand, as well as to reduce the risks of an authoritarian society), even if these preferences may be influenced, *inter alia*, by decisions in city planning. What is probably a more disturbing problem, for adherents of a pluralistic society, is the strength of various pressure groups, and the uneven distribution of propaganda resources in most societies, not just totalitarian ones.

I have hardly seen either in the old or in the New Left literature any attempts to design methods to find out what individual "needs" or preferences are. Instead of simply *neglecting* the problem of how information on needs and preferences may be derived, I think the revolutionary left should be *particularly* concerned with exactly these problems. When the leftists pretend to be able to determine not only consumer preferences as revealed by the market but also the "true" needs of consumers, they have set a much more difficult task for themselves than have the traditional economists. Moreover, how can the New Leftists be so sure that the preferences on which the decision-makers in the New Left world will base their decisions constitute a better approximation to the true or deep needs of the individuals than do the preferences revealed by the individuals themselves in their market behavior, after exposure to advertisement, public information, and debate?

POWER

It is probably correct to say, as asserted by the New Left, that economists have not extensively studied the problem of economic power and the power struggle between different groups in society. Some important insights about power are, however, given in economic analysis, concerning the power of monopolies and, in particular, the power of the state.

For instance, one of the main lessons to be drawn from economic analysis—theoretical as well as empirical—is that a pluralistic society presupposes a far-reaching decentralization of economic decisions—decisions about labor supply and consumption by individual households, as well as decisions by firms about production, investments, and prices. In particular, an extremely important achievement of economics is to show that a far-reaching decentralization in these respects can function, and hence that chaos does not emerge, by letting a market mechanism coordinate the decisions of millions of individuals, thereby avoiding an enormous central bureaucracy à la the Soviet Union. This achievement has, or should have, a profound importance for *all* discussions of economic and political power.

Unfortunately, this message has not been well understood by the New Left, whose adherents are simultaneously against *both* markets and a centralized bureaucracy. Moreover, the New Left is often in favor of decentralization in spite of its refusal to accept a market system. The inability of the New Left, as well as of Sweezy and Hymer-Roosevelt, to grasp these important points shows that traditional economics has not only an extremely important but also a very difficult message for the New Left regarding the problem of power. After all, this issue has been the basic message in economics from Adam Smith to Oscar Lange, Friedrich

Hayek, and the contemporary market socialists in Eastern Europe.

It is also interesting to note that the empirical evidence of history does not indicate that the problem of *abuse* of power would tend to disappear with the removal of private capitalism. Thus, it may be worthwhile for the New Left to reconsider the implications of collective ownership for the distribution of power in society. For instance, is it likely that the risk of a concentration of political, economic, and military power—with a military-industrial complex as a result—is really *smaller* in a society where the public authorities do not only cooperate with private defense industries, but also, in fact, *own* the defense industries? A very decentralized form of collective ownership would probably be necessary to reduce the risk. But then we are confronted with the question whether the political leaders in a socialist or communist society can be convinced that they should implement such a decentralization, implying a reduction in their own power. I am afraid that empirical evidence does not support the hypothesis that it is easy to decentralize power in economies based mainly on public ownership. A related issue is the opportunity for people outside the top state and party bureaucracy to take initiatives. (Sweezy obviously does not regard this problem as important, as he questions whether there is "any reasoned support for the view that innovation (in the areas of production) is a highly desirable characteristic of any economic system.")

Similar reflections apply to "conventional" economic analysis of the role of competition, which is not only a method of forcing prices down to marginal or average costs, of preventing firms from neglecting consumers, and of allowing entry of new firms, but also a way to limit the *power* of individual firms (whether private or public).

BASIC ISSUES NEGLECTED BY THE NEW LEFT

Sweezy and Hymer-Roosevelt not only argue that traditional economists and the revolutionary left are interested in different problems, but also hold the position that the revolutionary left need not concern itself with the problems dealt with by conventional economists. As Sweezy says: "The radical left has no reasons to 'entertain views' about problems of which 'neoclassical' economists are concerned." Or as Hymer-Roosevelt argue: "The New Left will not tolerate changing the questions."

On this point the New Left is dead wrong. The reason is, of course, that *every* economic system has to solve very much the same fundamental problems about information, incentives, coordination, allocation of resources, distribution of income, wealth, and economic power.

To highlight these general problems, I tried in my book to organize the discussion around six classical problems for economic systems: (1) the choice between markets and formalized administrative processes ("bureaucracy") as methods for providing information about preferences and technology, for allocating resources in accordance with these preferences, and for coordinating billions of decisions in order to make them reasonably consistent; (2) the choice between centralization and decentralization in the decision-making procedure; (3) the advantages and disadvantages of different forms of ownership, such as state, cooperative, and private ownership; (4) the possibility of using material incentives to bring about efficiency and to respect consumer preferences, without bringing about serious conflicts in the distribution of income and wealth; (5) the choice between competition, planning and collusion in operating firms; and (6) the meaning of "development."

Both Sweezy and Hymer-Roosevelt are quite silent on

these important points. The main reason for the neglect of these problems is probably that they are regarded by the New Left as *specific problems of capitalist societies.* I would reiterate that what in the revolutionary literature are regarded as specific problems of capitalist societies, and as resulting in "contradiction" in capitalist societies, are in fact *general* problems for *all* societies, particularly rich societies, as these have to build on a substantial division of labor. I would also suggest that the adherents of the revolutionary left are prevented from seeing this fact precisely because of their lack of deeper insights into the fundamental issues dealt with in (the best parts of) economics.

A few examples to illustrate the point follow. The first involves the use of knowledge; the second the role of incentives. A few further examples will be simply enumerated.

THE USE OF KNOWLEDGE IN SOCIETY[2]

We know that *knowledge* relevant for economic decisions within a nation, concerning consumption, investment, and production, is not only enormously large, but also extremely heterogeneous, fragmented, and partly subjective, the last especially in the case of consumer preferences. One of the basic problems—and maybe *the* fundamental problem—in economics is to find methods of using this decentralized and fragmented knowledge in an efficient way, in conformity with the interest of the individuals in the society. In a simple agrarian society, consisting of a number of isolated Robinson Crusoe-like enclaves without much contact with each other, most of these problems disappear because all relevant information about both production and consumption refers to conditions *within* the decision-making units

[2]The title of this section is borrowed from the title of Friedrich Hayek's famous article in the *American Economic Review,* xxxv (September, 1945), 519–530.

themselves. It would seem that much of New Left literature implicitly assumes that the problems about information, incentives, and coordination in industrial societies are basically not very different from those of Robinson Crusoe societies.

The fact is, of course, that in a highly industrialized society, the basic problem for each decision unit is precisely to obtain and adjust to information initially available *only outside* the decision-making unit itself, and that this is the background for the complicated problems of coordination with the "outside" world, i.e. with other decision-making units.

Sweezy, no doubt, gives the right connotations to the general notions in New Left literature when he visualizes a society of "communes which are social and political as well as economic units" rather than "firms or plants." Another typical vision of the New Left literature is Mandel's prescription for "self-management of free communes of producers and consumers, in which everybody will take it in turn to carry out administrative work, in which the difference between 'director' and 'directed' will be abolished, and a federation of which will eventually cover the whole world."[3] It seems to be nearly blasphemous when economists break into this idyllic picture asking, for instance: "How do you plan to run the steel industry?"

If this formulation should be interpreted as a desire to create rather small *self-sufficient* organizations, it certainly outlines a *theoretically* possible form of socioeconomic system. And if there are people in the present society who would like to live (a materially poor life) in such organizations, the rest of us should not prevent them from doing so. A problem, though, is that most adherents of these "com-

[3]Ernest Mandel, *Marxist Economic Theory*, Vol. 2 (New York: Monthly Review Press, 1968), p. 677.

mune models" show no signs of establishing such organizations for themselves; they instead seem to argue that *all of us* should live in that way.

There is also an obvious risk that this "commune" terminology helps to hide the basic problems of information, incentives, and coordination that any society with even a modest type of specialization has to solve—regardless of the ownership of the means of production. The fact is, of course, that the New Left, or Marxism for that matter, has no comprehensive theory about information, incentives, allocation, and coordination.[4] This is no *minor* lacuna in New Left economics, or in Marxism. It implies basically *the absence of economic theory*. Economics without a theory of information, incentives, allocation, and coordination is not like Hamlet without the Prince. It is not Hamlet at all.

INCENTIVES AND THE LABOR MARKET

Hymer-Roosevelt, in line with Marxist analysis, seem to imply that the freedom of the worker is highly limited by the existence of a labor market: "When the worker sells his labor he in fact surrenders his freedom." Obviously, Hymer-Roosevelt do *not* see wage differentials as a necessary incentive for efficiency and training or as a useful method of allocating labor to different jobs, *except* in capitalist societies: "We see them as necessary to the conservation of the capitalist mode of production." They also assert that in a non-capitalist society, in spite of the absence of individual

[4]This is partly admitted by one of the adherents of New Left economics, Howard Sherman, who writes: "For the most part, though, it is true that Marx did not emphasize demand, let alone changes in demand; nor did he consider in detail the problems of producing proportionate to that demand; nor did he consider all the related problems of choice among scarce resources and capital." My only objection to this statement is the words "in detail," which I think should be deleted. (*Radical Political Economy*, New York: Basic Books, 1972, p. 45.)

economic incentives, it will not be necessary to accept "competition, discipline, authoritarianism, rigid schedules."

What evidence has the New Left for these rather strong assertions? A traditional way of looking at the existence of a labor market is that it creates considerable *freedom* for the worker, at least if there is a high level of employment and there exist strong labor unions—particularly when we compare it to the alternative system that is necessary in economies without a "labor market": allocation of the workers to different jobs by orders and threat of punishment.

In fact, it would seem that (the best parts of) traditional economic literature give a rather good understanding of why a labor market, with wage differentials, provides an opportunity to combine a reasonably efficient allocation of resources with freedom of the individual to choose a job. I think that traditional theory also gives some understanding of the problems that occur in societies with a minimum use of economic incentives—problems illustrated in practice by the experiences of the Soviet Union during the 1930's; Germany in 1938–1943; and Cuba during the 1960's.

In considering the role of competition, I believe it is also worthwhile to think through whether every system where job positions are determined on the basis of individual competence, may not *automatically* become a rather "competitive society" for the individual, even if competition between "firms" or "communes" is minimal. Perhaps only a traditional "class society"—where everybody is born to his position—can minimize competition between individuals. (For instance, look at the hard, not to say cruel, competition between individual leaders and bureaucrats in the communist countries.)

As to the problems about "discipline," "authoritarianism," and "rigid schedules," it is at least *possible* that these phenomena have more to do with the existence of advanced technology and large-scale organizations than with capitalism. In fact, both theory and experience indicate that authoritarianism is the necessary outcome of the *absence* of a market system rather than of the *existence* of a market system, for reasons developed by "traditional" economists.

OTHER PROBLEMS NEGLECTED BY THE NEW LEFT

The list of problems that traditional economic theory deals with and that the New Left consistently tends to neglect is in fact practically unlimited. This is an important point not only because an analysis of these problems help us to understand the present society in the West, but also because they are *general* problems for *every* society. A short enumeration of some additional general issues may further clarify the point.

For instance, it may be that the dilemma of reconciling full employment and price stability exists in *all* societies with free labor market organization. It is instructive to see that inflation immediately tends to accelerate in societies where *some* modest decentralization in the labor market has been established, such as in Czechoslovakia and Yugoslavia during the sixties. It is also quite clear that every society is confronted with the problem of choosing a combination of present and future consumption, a problem highlighted in the literature on optimum growth paths. It would also seem that every society is confronted with the dilemma of finding a compromise between the economic differentials needed to give incentives and the desire for equality. Moreover, the difficulties of finding the demand curves for social goods, and of creating incentives for efficient provision of these goods, are hardly less in noncapitalist societies than in the present-day Western economies, as the share of such goods is supposed to be larger in the former. Similarly, the problem of whether public employees should be allowed to strike can hardly be less serious in societies where the public sector dominates the economy than in the present Western economies. In fact, the right to strike has often been denied in strongly nationalized societies. If employees had no wish to strike in these societies, such laws would hardly be necessary.

Similarly, problems posed by externalities are certainly general issues for *all* economic systems. In fact, an energetic policy for environmental protection may be "simpler" in societies where the behavior functions of the firms are rather unambiguous, such as dictated by profit maximization. In such systems all policies designed to make pollution more expensive will result in a clear-cut effect on the firms, discouraging polluting activities. It *might* in fact be *more* difficult to influence firms whose behavior pattern is less specific. An illustration is the experience in some countries in Eastern Europe, where fees for environmental destruction were introduced but did not result in any considerable reductions in pollution, possibly for the reason that the firms did not care very much if profits were reduced: they preferred to pay fees rather than change their production activities.

It is also interesting to notice that "excessive exploitation" of natural resources, a problem that has raised considerable interest in recent years, may in fact be *more* difficult to solve for firms that are not profit maximizing. We know that profit-maximizing firms have rather strong (though maybe not sufficiently strong) incentives to economize with raw materials in the production process. Firms that have been inclined to maximize *gross output,* as in Eastern Europe, on the other hand have incentives to use *too much* raw material —as illustrated by Khrushchev's complaints about "the steel eaters" in Soviet firms.

DETERMINISM VERSUS SMORGASBORD
An important point in Sweezy's paper is the alleged impossibility of reforming the capitalist system: "To speak of reforming capitalism is either naïveté or deception." The rea-

son would be that exploitation, inequality, revolutions, wars, financial crises, and catastrophe are "the inevitable outcome of capitalism's inner contradictions." We are told that it is wrong to believe that "from now on anything can happen." The future is, we are told, not "a kind of smorgasbord offering all the dishes in the liberal cookbook from which 'we' can choose those which most appeal to us."

It is an old insoluble philosophical issue: to what extent human beings, by concerted action, can choose their own future. It is possible that we reformists overstate the possibilities of choosing the future by deliberate actions in the context of a mixed economy. Maybe the technical, economic, and social "forces" are more difficult to tame than most of us want to believe, in spite of the fact that much of the content of today's mixed economy, with its welfare state, certainly is the result of deliberate political decisions by democratically elected parliaments.

But if deliberate reforms, as Sweezy suggests, are impossible in capitalist societies, why does all determinism disappear when we enter the socialist society? Why are there no "inevitable laws" in such societies? Why can anything happen there?

For instance, it does not seem self-evident that the huge bureaucracy in the Soviet Union is a historical accident that can be avoided in other nonmarket societies, now that "the negative lessons" have been learned by the radical left. It is at least *possible*, as I have tried to argue in my book, that the all-powerful bureaucracy in the Soviet Union is a logical consequence of the attempts to minimize the reliance on markets and competition. This hypothesis at least is firmly anchored in economic theory and empirical facts. And maybe it is at least *possible* that decentralization of economic initiative is difficult to bring about in societies with only one owner of the capital, even if this owner happens to be the government itself. It is also *possible* that the seizure of power by force easily results in a selection of leaders that may be both authoritarian and cruel. Maybe there are "inevitable laws" of revolution. And maybe there are also "inevitable laws" of bureaucracies—for instance "Parkinson-like laws"—as much as there are inevitable laws of market systems with private ownership. One law that *certainly* exists is that an industrialized nonmarket economy, based on division of labor, has to be a highly centralized and bureaucratized society.

In other words, why are the "regressions, cruelties, and tragedies" (to quote Sweezy) following many socialist revolutions just historical accidents, when Sweezy is so sure that tragedies in capitalist societies are *not* accidents, but necessary outcomes of a capitalist economic system? Is there any logical or philosophical basis for this complete shift of philosophy regarding the driving forces of historical development, simply because there has been a transfer of ownership of the means of production from one group of people to another?

Why is it so self-evident that there is a "smorgasbord to choose from" in societies with one type of ownership but not in another?

FINAL WORDS

Why should professional economists interest themselves in "the political economy" of the New Left? It is obviously not because of the intellectual level of the New Left writings on economic issues; this level is in general very low indeed. Rhetoric is to an enormous extent substituted for analysis. However, there are, I think, some important reasons why economists should take the New Left literature quite seriously.

The first one is that the New Left literature is taken seriously by a large number of young people, mainly university students, above all in countries with reasonably great freedom to read and to speak, and future society may very well be considerably influenced by what the present generation of students thinks and believes. Maybe we should again remember the celebrated quotation from Keynes: "The ideas of economists and political philosophers, both when they are right and when they are wrong, are more powerful than is usually understood. Indeed the world is ruled by little else." And, after all, we, or at least our children, have to live in the same society as the New Left people.

Second, the New Left has reminded us, as citizens, of a number of "eternal" problems about society and politics—issues of the distribution of income and power, ownership, externalities, public participation, and social values in general (the quality of life)—aspects that many established people in the ordinary pursuit of work may easily forget.

Third, the New Left has challenged the economists to do better research in a number of underdeveloped fields in the social sciences, and has helped to remind us of the risks of drawing the borders of our subject too narrowly, which might have been an effect of the neoclassical and Keynesian revolutions.

The New Left has also forced us to reconsider whether some parts of the Marxian tradition are worth integrating into the "traditional" tool-box of economic analysis. For instance, it may be important to concede to the Marxian insistence that competition between *groups* of people—"classes" —should be given more consideration in the social sciences, rather than concentrating the analysis on individual behavior. The insistence that interdisciplinary approaches may be fruitful for an understanding of many important problems is probably also well taken (of course, this is not a specific Marxian view!). It is also quite true that Marxism has a theory of long-term historical development—a philosophy of history—which most economists have not bothered to deal with. When so many students *demand* theories, or speculations, about long-term historical development, should not social scientists respect these revealed "consumer preferences" by helping to supply knowledge, views, and speculations in this field? Even if it is impossible at this stage to supply very *good* theories, maybe it is enough if they improve upon those presented à la Hegel, Marx, Spencer, Toynbee, etc.

On the other hand, it is necessary to prove to the New Left, as well as to other citizens, that traditional economics is a powerful tool for understanding fundamental problems in existing and conceivable societies—in fact, in my opinion, the *most* powerful tool available. Thereby, it may be possible to show the New Left that many problems that they regard as the "inevitable outcome" of capitalism, or of the mixed economy, are in fact much more interesting than that: they are usually *general* problems to be faced in *all* economic systems.

RADICAL ECONOMICS: A REVIEW ESSAY
Robert L. Heilbroner

NEW SCHOOL FOR SOCIAL RESEARCH

THIS LUCID analysis of contemporary radical thought is an effort to present both a sympathetic portrayal and a reasoned criticism of the doctrines of the New Left. As Paul Samuelson points out in his admiring introduction, Professor Lindbeck has a special qualification for this task that would be difficult to find in an American student or professor, embroiled as partisan or embattled as foe, in the currents of New Left political economics. This special qualification is that of being a foreigner, an outsider. Like Myrdal or de Tocqueville, Lindbeck approaches the problem from a "neutral" position, *au delà de la mêlée.*

What Samuelson fails to note, however, is that Lindbeck is not *audessus de la mêlée,* for the ideas and criticisms of radical economics are an international rather than a strictly American phenomenon. However benign and impartial Lindbeck may have felt during his visits to M.I.T., Columbia, and Berkeley during the troubled year 1968–69, he brings to his analysis the preconceptions and premises of a Swedish social democrat whose economic philosophy is under the same assault in his own country as it is here. Perhaps that is why Lindbeck has produced a critique that, for all its sympathetic ear and patient tone, seems to me somehow to miss the point of much of the New Left's attack, and therefore to answer it in a way that the proponents of radical views will not find convincing.

Lindbeck sets himself two principal tasks: first, to distill the essence of the New Left arguments against contemporary

Reprinted from *The American Political Science Review,* September, 1972, pp. 1017–1020.

neoclassical (the truer word would be nonclassical) economics; and second, to formalize the charges brought by the New Left not against economics as such, but against the economic system itself. Lindbeck sifts five basic arguments against neoclassical economics from the writings of the left.[1] They are:

1. Conventional economics tends to underestimate the importance of the question of income distribution—the pivotal issue for Ricardo, Mill, and Marx. Furthermore, when

[1] It is perhaps invidious to single out individual works from the monographs, books, pamphlets, and articles that constitute the literature in which Lindbeck is interested, particularly since Lindbeck's book is anything but an *ad hominem* attack. Nonetheless, it may help the reader orient himself if I identify a few books and individuals mentioned by Lindbeck as constituting spokesmen (not *the* spokesmen) for the doctrines he has set out to analyze. There is, of course, a central group whose ideas derive essentially from Marxian writing or philosophy: here we find the well-known works of Baran and Sweezy (especially *Monopoly Capital*), or Herbert Marcuse (*One Dimensional Man*). But the group is by no means exclusively Marxist. It includes rightwing anarchists such as Angus Black (*A Radical's Guide to Economic Reality*), and liberal disestablishmentarians such as J. K. Galbraith (*The New Industrial State*). Not mentioned by Lindbeck, but extremely important as current contributors to New Left thought are a group of well-trained economists out of Harvard and MIT and other bastions of respectability. Many of them belong to the Union for Radical Political Economics (URPE), and their writings will be found in the publications of that organization, in periodicals such as the *Monthly Review, Ramparts,* and other journals of the left; in various "readers," often of an eclectic cast; and occasionally in the hallowed pages of the sacred journals of the profession itself. Merely as a suggestive sampling let me mention: *Economics, Mainstream Readings and Radical Critiques* (ed. David Mermelstein); *Radical Political Economy* by Howard Sherman; *Up Against the American Myth,* written and edited by Tom Christoffel, David Finkelhor and Dan Gilbarg; *Problems in Political Economy: an Urban Perspective,* ed. David Gordon. This listing ignores numerous important— often somewhat technical papers by Herbert Gintis, Arthur MacEwan, Tom Weisskopf, and Stephen Marglin of Harvard; by Edward J. Nell and Stephen Hymer of the New School: by Michael Zweig of Stony Brook; John Gurley of Stanford; and, as the saying goes, much much more.

the question *is* studied, neoclassical analysis interests itself only in marginal issues, such as wage differentials based on skill, education, etc, while sidestepping the fundamental question of the division of income among *classes*.

2. Neoclassical economics develops a detailed analysis of resource allocation in response to consumer preferences, but takes the preferences of consumers as "given" rather than as a matter for investigation and explanation.

3. Conventional economics is absorbed by quantitative problems to the exclusion of qualitative ones. (I recently heard a New Left quip that sums up this criticism in a nutshell: "Capitalism is a system that transforms quality into quantity.")

4. The neoclassicists study changes at the margin but not changes in the totality. They consider economics to be the study of the variables of a given system, not of its parameters.

5. Conventional economics overlooks the interaction of economic and political processes. Indeed, its chief difficulty is that it prides itself on being "economics" and not "political economy," thereby implying that it deals with relationships that are in some sense transhistoric. (Probably no remark so raises the hackles of the radical as the statement that economics can be defined as "the theory of choice.")

Lindbeck finds a grain of truth in each of these charges, and sometimes more than a grain. Conventional economics, he admits, *is* often small-scale in its focus and concerns: excessively technicized; indifferent to or afraid of questions involving social structure; and blind to social malfunction until that malfunction has been discovered by someone else —instances being the "discovery" of poverty by Michael Harrington, of imperialism by Magdoff and other nonconventional writers, of ecology by the Sierra Club, of the military economy by Seymour Melman, of corporate and regulatory misperformance by Ralph Nader. Hence his tone is conciliatory. But his judgment stops short of endorsing the radical attack on neoclassical economics as a sterile or apologistic pursuit. Rather, Lindbeck seeks to demonstrate that neoclassical economics in fact possesses the "tools" to investigate and clarify these problems, and that its failures must therefore be chalked up to whatever social processes or pressures have diverted the main body of the profession away from serious matters, rather than to any fundamental shortcomings of the discipline itself.

Is this defense well taken? I do not think that Lindbeck makes as strong a case for his contention as he believes. With regard to the question of income distribution, for example, he cites as support for the capabilities of neoclassical economics recent studies by Gary Becker and Jacob Mincer, although this is precisely the sort of work attacked by the New Left because it begins from assumptions whose legitimacy they question. In particular, the radical economists attack the validity of two key concepts in all neoclassical explanations of income distribution, asking whether "marginal productivity" in fact measures anything that can (or should) be used as a criterion for analyzing income shares, and disputing the much-touted idea of "human capital" because it swallows whole the very concept—capital—that needs to be criticized.

Lindbeck is more favorably inclined toward argument (2) —the neoclassical assumption that tastes are autonomous— and merely cautions against naive generalizations about the ease with which tastes may be formed or manipulated. This caution is fully justified. But Lindbeck fails to respond to the underlying thrust of the New Left critique—that *all* tastes in a society dominated by the imperatives of a commercial civilization are in some deep manner suspect. Although few radicals claim to know what the "natural" tastes of men are or should be, they call into question the basic acquiesence of conventional economics before the conception of a "utility-maximizing" world, and its indifference to the socioeconomic preconditions for such a world.

The quality of life—criticism (3)—is, as Lindbeck says, a problem to which conventional economics has until recently paid little heed. His reply to the New Left criticism is that there is now an "interesting and growing" literature in which various methods of dealing with externalities are examined. Here Lindbeck misses two points. A large portion of the New Left critique with regard to the quality of life has to do with the alienation of men under conditions of industrial labor and intensive consumer pressure: Lindbeck does not acknowledge the virtual absence of any matching concern within conventional economics. Further, with respect to the problem of externalities proper, the New Left is interested not merely in the existence of externalities or the presence of economic tools, such as taxes, regulation, or subsidies, to minimize them. It is interested in detecting within the class of problems having to do with externalities that subset whose roots lie in the specific drives and constraints of capitalism. It is no doubt true that the New Left often confuses the general problems of industrial pollution with the special problems of capitalist pollution; but it is also true that conventional economics pays little or no heed to special kinds of environmental damage that are directly traceable to the specific forms of production dictated by capitalist institutions.

I shall bypass Lindbeck's treatment of the fourth point—he grants that economists have not been much interested in large-scale historical processes or in comparative economic systems—and focus on the last question: the problem of economics versus political economy.

Here Lindbeck again seems to miss the meaning of the New Left criticism. He admits that economists have not paid much attention to such problems as lobbying or the means by which special groups win special privileges. He grants as well that little attention has been paid to the interaction between domestic interests and foreign policy—in short, imperialism. His countercriticism is that the methods used by the New Left to examine these questions are inadequate—a mixture of vulgar Marxism, mechanical linkages of the "interests" of big business and the state, etc. What is needed, he suggests, is empirical work that will cut through these theoretical misconceptions to study the precise means "by which various domestic pressure groups obtain privileges through economic and other types of legislation and of how foreign domination may sometimes occur through foreign investments, foreign aid, trade policies, military policies, and the like."

Who can fault such a prescription? The problem is, can it be filled by the present ideas of neoclassical economics? Can conventional economists explain the existence or the stubborn persistence of the upper tail of the Lorenz curve of income distribution, despite "progressive" taxation? Can it explain why international trade, the theory of which promises that exchange will yield benefits to both parties, has resulted in the polarization of a highly developed and a highly underdeveloped world? Can it account for the persistence of poverty despite the supposedly curative effects of growth? I fear the answer to these questions is No. I would agree with Lindbeck that the New Left often explains these and other aspects of socioeconomic reality in ways that strike me as tendentious or simply wrong. But at least the problems are faced. They are not faced by the majority of conventional economists. Moreover there is little evidence that the "tools" of conventional theory will unravel problems whose difficulty is that they are not problems of "economics" but of political economy.

The second section of Lindbeck's book, in which he deals with the New Left's criticism of the economy, is stronger and more thought-provoking than the first. Rather than enumerate Lindbeck's summary of the New Left's objections to the economic system, let me concentrate on one issue that repeatedly surfaces in this portion of the book. This is a pointed emphasis on a "contradiction" in which the New Left finds itself by virtue of its opposition to two aspects of contemporary society. As Lindbeck puts it:

> One characteristic feature of the New Left movement is that most of its adherents are strongly opposed to markets. In the literature of the New Left, a market system is denounced as primitive, inefficient, chaotic, antisocial, unfair, and basically immoral.
> One problem with this position is that most of the New Left's writers in this field are also strongly opposed to bureaucracy, that is, to formalized hierarchical administration. For instance, the bureaucracy in the Soviet Union is often criticized in New Left literature. . . . It may be possible to make a strong case against either markets or administrative systems, but if we are against *both* we are in trouble; there is hardly a third method for allocating resources and coordinating economic decisions, if we eliminate physical force. Both markets and administrative procedures may, of course, take many different forms. Markets may be more or less competitive and administrative procedures more or less centralized, with some decision-making by vote, and so on. *Thus, the more strongly we are against bureaucracy, the more we should be in favor of markets.* (pp. 32–33, italics in text).

Lindbeck's thrust is a shrewd one, but I am made somewhat uneasy by the use he makes of it. For one thing, he is not technically correct in asserting that market/bureaucracy is an either/or proposition. The mode of production and distribution in primitive societies is regulated by an internalized self-discipline called *tradition;* and it is entirely possible that some form of communitarian socialism might rely on the same mechanism in the future. Indeed, as Samuelson says in his introduction, the "utopian self-sufficient kibbutz" *is* an alternative to both market and bureaucracy.

Then, too, I am unhappy at Lindbeck's failure to take seriously his own qualifying phrase that "markets may be more or less competitive and administrative procedures more or less centralized" (p. 33). Throughout the remainder of the text we are faced with the dilemma of market or bureaucracy without the shadings that may make this choice in fact a good deal less decisive or contradictory than Lindebck implies. For example, Lindbeck does not differentiate between the market for *goods*, which many New Left critics would accept, at least for a provisional period, and that for labor, which most (but not all) radicals would not accept, certainly under the ground rules of property rights. In addition, Lindbeck does not raise for our consideration the possibilities of tempering bureaucracy through reforms that go in the Yugoslav or Chinese directions. Although we have almost no detailed knowledge of the effectiveness of these efforts, there is no doubt that both nations are trying to avoid the monolith of Sovietism that Lindbeck unconsciously makes the sole paradigm of bureaucratic allocation. Thus we are faced with a false choice in his iron dichotomy, and his clear preference for a market solution results more from his opposition to an oversimplified ideal type of bureaucracy than from a careful discussion of possible alternatives.

It must be clear that I have serious doubts about the effectiveness of Lindbeck's counterarguments to the New Left. Yet I would be doing his book a considerable injustice if I were to leave the reader with an impression only of its weaknesses. Terse and often penetrating, Lindbeck's essay reminds me in its simplicity and clarification of Robert Dahl's *After the Revolution?* In both books, the puzzles and difficulties that slogans hide from us are ruthlessly dragged out for examination. I can only applaud when Lindbeck stresses the blurred correlation between the structure of ownership on the one hand and political and social conditions on the other (Sweden and the Union of South Africa both rest atop a base of private property and market relations). I am impressed by his discussion of the costs of obtaining information in a marketless society and with the social results of failing to do so. I am struck (as is Samuelson) by his telling critique of Galbraith's theory of demand-creation.

Most important of all is Lindbeck's function in pointing out to the New Left the tasks to which it must sooner or later address itself. Judging by the radical literature with which I am familiar, the New Left is almost entirely concerned with criticism, not program. Yet, as Lindbeck points out:

> As all serious scholars know, the real problems start *after* the revolution or, what from this point of view is about the same thing, *without* a revolution. However there is very little, if any, discussion in the literature of the New Left about the *methods* of solving the problems which chiefly worry economists, such as the reconciliation of full employment with price stability and equilibrium in the balance of payments; the determination of an optimal growth rate and hence an optimal combination of consumption today and consumption tomorrow . . . ; the design of a workable compromise between the income differentials needed to give incentives for work and for the allocation of the labor force, and the desire for equality; . . . whether employees in the public sector should have the right to strike; . . . how to avoid an enormous concentration of power in a small group of politicians and administrators in a society with growing government intervention; . . . the advantages and disadvantages of multinational firms; whether important decisions of social and economic policy can really be efficiently carried out by the national state. . . . On most of these difficult and important problems the New Left is quite silent or superficial (pp. 98–99).

The indictment is a powerful one—until one asks whether conventional economics is not also silent or superficial before most of these issues. Thus once again, Lindbeck's book is not quite the "outsider's" view that it claims to be. The danger is therefore that its clear and calm exposition will be taken by the neoclassical economist as a definitive answer to questions and problems to which it does not, in fact, do full justice. Nonetheless, Lindbeck could perform an invaluable service if he would motivate members of the New Left to address themselves to the sorts of issues he raises in the paragraph quoted above. I rather suspect, however, that if these problems are to be examined with the care they deserve, it will not be until they are raised with the same degree of clarity and urgency by someone who is an insider unwilling to postpone the agenda of the future until the revolution brings it home with stunning force.

THE POLITICAL ECONOMY OF THE NEW RIGHT

Bruce McFarlane

THE AUSTRALIAN NATIONAL UNIVERSITY

INTRODUCTION

A COMPETENT COUNTERATTACK on the recent upsurge of dissatisfaction with orthodox economics has been overdue. Moreover, the case for market systems has needed strengthening as the passion and insights of Von Mises, Von Hayek, and Erhardt have been fading into obscurity. However, a restatement of the case for market mechanisms had to be a wide-ranging one. Milton Friedman, for example, is perhaps too narrowly focused on money markets to serve as a rallying point for the "New Right." As well, some bows in the direction of those capitalist societies which have engaged in a reduction of social injustice could only strengthen a modern, more streamlined defense of orthodox economics and the capitalist system which it explains and defends.

The New Right has found such a restatement and a new spokesman with impeccable credentials. He is Mr. Assar Lindbeck, a young but influential Swedish economist, a member of the Nobel Prize Committee for Economics, an adviser to Swedish banks, disciple of P. A. Samuelson, and formerly a close associate of the leftist Prime Minister of Sweden, Olof Palme. It must be said at once that Lindbeck is not one of the troglodytes of laissez-faire, and that he does not maintain that all planning for social purpose is necessarily irrational. It remains true, however, that his approach is saturated with the presumption of the superiority of the market system, of commodity production over

Reprinted from *The Review of Radical Political Economics* (URPE), Summer 1972.

all other institutional arrangements for an economy; that he elevates optimality in resource allocation and "economic efficiency" (as traditionally defined in the orthodox text-books) to the status of a golden yardstick; and that this prism condemns both socialist economies and New Left economists to the original sin of irrationality.

To this point Lindbeck sounds like any ordinary neo-classical economist criticizing the New Left. Nevertheless his book is deserving of close study for the Swedish-style, social-democratic gloss given to economic issues, the concessions about pollution and various failings of the market economy, and its quarrels with New Left writers on these points. Again, this is perhaps the most comprehensive and intelligent counterattack that has been produced; since it is being widely recommended as an essential reference to the Right Wing backlash element, it is worth perusing.

What are the basic ideas in it? I will discuss these under a number of headings: (a) defense of orthodox economic theory against "New Left" attack; (b) Lindbeck's view of the bureaucratic society as the *inevitable* alternative to the market economy; (c) his novel critique of centrally planned economies of the Soviet type; (d) the notion that the market is the *only* effective antibureaucratic economic force.

A DEFENSE OF ORTHODOX ECONOMICS

Lindbeck quite clearly sees that the main thrust of the growing criticism of Samuelson-type economics underlines its irrelevance on large social questions and neglect of the power structure of society. He lists major charges under five headings and tries to meet them in turn. In these pages we get the best parts of the book under review. Lindbeck is clearly at home with technical microeconomic and welfare economic theory in a way that he is not when he ventures into political or social theory.

The five major criticisms reviewed in *Political Economy of the New Left* are: (i) too little attention is paid to quality of life problems; (ii) economic theory is too static and too concerned with static allocation problems; (iii) economists have excessively neglected the problems of distribution of wealth, income and economic power; (iv) obsession with marginal problems rather than structural or qualitative changes in the economic system; (v) neglect of problems arising from the interaction of political and economic factors.

(i) While maintaining that the problem of priorities in the choice of topics to be studied by economists is one of "subjective evaluations," Lindbeck concedes that too little effort has gone into the "qualitative" and "distributional" aspects of economic life. However, he sees this mainly as an aberration of the 1950's, and maintains that over the last decade "research has expanded just in the neglected areas emphasized by the new left." Here he underlines the Garry Becker–Jacob Mincer analysis of human capital (including the explanation of income distribution by differing returns to education); the expansion of welfare economics (by Baumol, P. Bohm, etc.) to examine the external effects on environment; and the growing literature on comparative economic systems. And as an example of a social scientist who integrates economic, social, and political factors in analysis, he cites his countryman, Gunnar Myrdal. (He does not mention however that Myrdal is everywhere attacked as not being a "pure" economist, that his *Asian Drama* was criticized for doing just this kind of integration—including in the *Swedish Journal of Economics,* nor that Myrdal's important *Challenge to World Poverty* has been universally ignored by economists and not least in Sweden itself.)

(ii) The author recognizes as quite damaging the charge that too much orthodox economics is confined to partial equilibrium analysis, but he says "it is less clear how efficient research in this field could be achieved . . . both the ultraliberal notion of the basic autonomy of individual preferences, and its opposite, the notion of the manipulated consumer, have great hopes of surviving for a long time to come."

What is surprising here is that Lindbeck nowhere mentions the work of professional economists who have tried to break out of partial analysis. There is, for example, Kalecki's work, which links the theory of the firm to the macroeconomic trends in the economy. There is the dynamic quasi-rent analysis suggested by Joan Robinson in her account of Euler's theorem. Above all, there is the treatment by Robin Marris and others of the growth of a firm seeking sales and development, rather than simple profit-maximization. The main liberating concept here is that the analyst does not accept market prices as being immutable facts. Lindbeck does refer scornfully to Galbraith on "manipulation" of markets, but nowhere does he himself face up to the erosion of partial analysis by the facts of monopoly. Perhaps generalizing from Swedish experience he simply assumes free international trade breaks up monopoly.

(iii) Another example of "Swedish blinkers" may be seen in the author's discussion of the treatment of income distribution by economists. He says that personal income distribution may have been relatively neglected since 1945, but that it was extensively analyzed during the first two decades of this century in connection with the theory and policy of taxation and public finance. But was it? Two Swedish economists—Knut Wicksell and Eric Lindahl—certainly made famous contributions, but who else was there? And how much of it got into the textbooks? It was not till Dalton, under the impact of the 1945-48 "common man" revolt in Britain, wrote his small textbook that students were systematically encouraged to take up this question. The rest had to turn to Maurice Dobb—the only Marxist economist in Britain before World War II. Lindbeck is also, it seems to me, overly sanguine about the marginal productivity theory of (factor) distribution. It is true that in the hands of Wicksell, it was shown how radical policy conclusions could be derived from Euler's theorem as applied to factor distribution—namely, that the workers did *not* get their marginal productivity during their peak working years and should be compensated in later life by more generous pensions. But outside of this, the only important non-Swedish *theoretical* contribution that could have actually helped the welfare of large masses of people was the prewar book by H.D. Dickinson—*Institutional Revenue.* Lindbeck does not mention this work. If he had read it, he might not have been so condescending about theories stressing "institutional arrangements" which he thinks have not been "rigorously developed."

(iv) On the question of the "small adjustments" complaint, Lindbeck concedes that "this type of criticism of the choice of topics makes good sense" and hopes for more from the growing field of comparative economic systems. But this is no answer at all; Lindbeck has shifted his ground from a promise to answer the question about "marginal changes within a given economic system" to a defense about "choice of topic" which is something quite separate.

Moreover, this logic of Lindbeck's does *not* meet the point made by new left economists (e.g., Zweig) about the implicit *epistemology* beneath this mode of thinking in small adjustments to the periphery of some large aggregate. This is that intellectual activity has no capacity to consider *total* change, the transformation of a *totality* of social relation. This guarantees that economic thinking will preserve the *status quo* by gradual reforms. This is what new left economists mean by the "complicity" between economic theory and contemporary capitalism, rather than some conspiracy view involving payment by business to "whitewash" corporate capitalism. It is not the simplistic view, as interpreted by Lindbeck, that "marginal analysis is even regarded as anti-revolutionary" which the New Left emphasizes.

(v) Most people would agree that New Left critiques have contributed to a fuller understanding of pollution and other damage to ecology and life. But again Lindbeck comes to the rescue: "The politician is more to blame than economic theory." In fact, says Lindbeck, "economic theory has dealt quite extensively with problems of external effects such as pollution and city blight," although he suggests that "it is high time the (dynamic version of) the Walrasian general system of economic analysis be connected with the ecological equilibrium system of our natural environment." But how useful *has* economic theory been on "external effects?" In America, the leading authority is probably R. H. Coase, who opposes even the minimal step of taxing the polluter to subsidize those suffering damage from pollution. In Sweden, the only economist in this field, P. Bohm, is a laissez-faire man and concluded, in his major article,[1] that the number of cases where welfare is improved by taxing polluters is very rare indeed. An honorable exception is W. J. Baumol, but his conclusions are neutral in regard to the price-mechanism as such. Is it any wonder that younger economists are less than satisfied with what has been written since Pigou on these increasingly urgent problems affecting the lives of large masses of people?

[1] P. Bohm, article in *Swedish Journal of Economics*, June 1970. In an article "Pollution Purification et Théorie des Effects Externes," published in *Annales de L'INSEE*, January–April 1970, p. 7, he even claimed that the losses incurred by the public as a consequence of the pollution of a lake can be evaluated in terms of the cost of transportation to the nearest unpolluted lake!

There is another basic issue involved, though, in Lindbeck's defense of orthodox economics. At the core of his approach is his belief that "objective research" is possible in social science, that "the advances made in recent years in testing with the help of non-experimental data have . . . narrowed the margins for subjective beliefs" so that the death risk for wrong theories has been greatly increased. Here he ignores what Thomas Kuhn has taught us about the nature of discovery in social sciences, to say nothing of Myrdal who not only maintains that research in the social sciences *is* subjective and based on political values, but especially singles out economics which "branched off from philosophy (which continued to be radical) and whose development until this day must largely be explained as determined by the felt need to isolate and render innocuous radical policy premises."[2]

Lindbeck, then, stands with contemporary economic theory in its claim to be a value-free and objective study relying on mathematical models to generate predictions that can be confirmed (or not) by empirical testing. Confronted with this claim some New Left economists certainly have failed to deal with it adequately. Some have simply said that economics fails to deal with basic contradictory structures of capitalism and others do not dispute the validity of the economist's box of conceptual tools but do not like its application to support repressive elements in society.

However, there is a better reply to Lindbeck: that even if he had perfectly captured the spirit of New Left criticisms of economic theory and technically refuted them, he has still missed a basic issue that was made by Marx and is implicit in Sweezy and Baran: that the function of critical

[2]Gunnar Myrdal, "The Place of Values in Social Policy," *Journal of Social Policy* (Cambridge), January 1972. See also Myrdal's interview "No Diplomacy in Social Science," *Ceres*, March 1971.

theory is to reveal the process by which social consciousness becomes distorted under capitalist relations and from
this to see the immanent concrete possibilities contained by
the system. The role of economics here is that of *mystification*, and a critique of it does not argue (as do Lindbeck
and some New Left economists) about concrete conditions
only, but also attacks the epistemological terrain from which
ideological notions emerge. A number of economists (including Myrdal) can claim to have done this, but they are *not*
answered by Lindbeck who keeps to the concrete and the
status quo—examining "deficiencies" but *never* the epistemological terrain.

POLITICAL ANALYSIS OF BUREAUCRACY AND MARXISM
Lindbeck entitled his essay "Political Economy" of the New
Left. He realizes that political analysis and ideology under-
pin the appraisals made by Gorz, Mandel, Sweezy, and others
of modern capitalism. Yet the author is unable to respond
to the Left on these terms and ends up judging their contributions solely against the yardsticks of social democratic
practice in Scandinavia or against the canons of orthodox
textbook economics. Where he does venture into comments
on political theory—for example, of Marx and Marcuse—his
views require vigorous rebuff for they are plausible while
being highly misleading.

We may begin by noting his incredibly simplistic treatment of *bureaucracy*. His view of bureaucracy is of the
"army of civil servants" genre; he does not see bureaucracy
as a social phenomenon. He says, for example: "related to
this neglect is the notion that the bureaucracy in the Soviet
Union is regarded almost as an unfortunate 'accident'
brought about by the wishes of bureaucrats and the idiosyncracies of particular individuals such as Lenin, or, more
often, Stalin. In fact, so far as I understand, the large

bureaucracy in the Soviet Union, although not necessarily all methods used by it, is an unavoidable consequence of the attempts to replace markets by administrative decisions." This statement reveals an appalling ignorance of the approach to bureaucracy taken by Trotsky and his followers (e.g., Mandel), to say nothing of Djilas' version in his "New Class" approach, which is quite similar in its main outlines. Here, the bureaucracy is *not* seen as an "accident" or as a result of the need to have an army of white-collar workers to replace market spontaneity, but as a social caste which has its roots in the control of nationalized property made possible by the decimation of cadres in the civil war and the failure to develop democratic decision-making techniques in industry and planning. Both Trotsky and Djilas see the bureaucracy as playing a social role far beyond the day-to-day administration of the economy and they also relate its historical growth to economic backwardness and the absence of a prerevolutionary entrepreneurial class.

Lindbeck does not even seem to be aware of the orthodox definitions of bureaucracy taught in any undergraduate School of Political Science—"traditional," "charismatic," and "legal rational" (i.e., a modern bureaucracy with regular promotion procedures, etc.). Presumably a follower of Weber would say that Russia has moved from a "traditional" bureaucracy (the Czarist regime) through its "charismatic" bureaucracy (under Stalin) to its modern system which approaches the legal-rational. Here Lindbeck's analysis is as pedestrian as it is possible to be. No wonder, then, that he goes on to complain that "this notion, that the State would 'wither away' in a system where resources would no longer be allocated by markets but in fact by Public administrative processes, is one of the most puzzling ideas in the history of economic and political doctrine." Marx on the Paris Commune and even Lenin in his writings on Worker's

Control (to say nothing of Kardelj and Tito in modern Yugoslavia) have always been quite clear on what is involved in the withering away of the State: that self-management in enterprises and other social organizations gradually replaces centralist, etatist direction, while centralized parliaments are replaced by the growing social and political power of communes.

However, it is when we turn to Lindbeck's treatment of Marcuse and Marx that the really fundamental gaps in his political analysis become even clearer.

Herbert Marcuse is Lindbeck's particular *bête-noir*. Attacks on him are used to discredit the New Left as a whole, and such attacks are very frequent in Lindbeck's book. Yet he disarmingly admits that there is a great deal of criticism of Marcuse in New Left literature, particularly for that writer's pessimism about the role of worker movements for the future transformation of society.

His first complaints are about Marcuse on "repressive tolerance," and he concludes that "obviously this way of arguing is very close to the general attack on western democracy by totalitarian movements and parties during the twentieth century." Lindbeck's interpretation of "repression" by the top economic and political circles of modern, bourgeois societies is a very, very, narrow one.[3] Moreover, apart from the *ad hominen* statement by Lindbeck above, his comments reveal no realization that "repressive tolerance" is used by Marcuse in a definite scientific way. It is used in a neo-Freudian sense, and its meaning is quite clearly explained in Marcuse's *Eros and Civilization*. But Lindbeck "vulgarizes" his critique of Marcuse, as for example when he says: "Maybe this is what Herbert Marcuse means when he talks about the remarkable capacity of con-

[3]Richard Goodwin, "The Social Theory of Herbert Marcuse," *The Atlantic*, June 1971, p. 6.

temporary society of containing social change, to reconcile the forces opposing the system and the integration of opposites."

Much of Lindbeck's other comments on Marcuse are taken up with the related theme: the use of advertising to influence consumers and interfere with the rationality of consumers' sovereignty. But in Lindbeck's eyes, "irrational" becomes the simplistic notion of manipulation by ad-men, which, he says, is absurdly exaggerated by Marcuse. But Lindbeck has failed to grasp the concepts of "irrational" and "false desires" used by Marcuse. As Richard Goodwin has pointed out:[4] "Marcuse argues that the statement that the U.S. consumers want automobiles is false in the special sense that such a statement does not examine the basis of that desire. It may be that Americans want automobiles because we have created cities from which a car is the only escape. Such a society is irrational; so although the view that most want an auto is a fact it is false to the extent that it is imposed by a society which itself is irrational and unfree." However, any such subtleties about Marcuse's use of the concept of irrational consumption completely escape Lindbeck, as do the complexities of "false wants."

He is in similar difficulties about Marcuse and dialectical thinking. In essence the use of a dialectical approach to modern capitalism is to evaluate it from the viewpoint of the alternatives it precludes. This is how Marcuse proceeds. He says that over the horizon there is another kind of society, another way of doing things that can bring us to the ideal of freedom. But in Lindbeck's hands this becomes a plea for "comparative economic systems" to be studied! What else can we make of the following passage in Lindbeck:

[4]Ibid.

Economists are in fact criticized for too much neglect of the important but difficult fields of comparative economic systems—to quote Herbert Marcuse: "in order to identify and define the possibilities of an optimal development, the critical theory must abstract from the actual organization and utilization of society's resources."

And with Marx and Marxism there is again mystification and vulgarization. He begins by noting the influence of "alienation" (as found in the writings of the younger Marx) on the New Left movement. He links it with "the desire for self-realization of the individual" which is frustrated by degrading monotonous work, causing dissatisfaction. However, this refers only to one of Marx's *four* categories of alienation, that of *private* alienation. Nowhere does Lindbeck refer to Marx (or Hegel) on *social alienation*: the concept that economic life is not a means to social life, but has become its dominating end. Thus, if every worker had an automobile and washing machine and annual holidays his personal feeling of distress or alienation could be drastically reduced, yet social alienation would continue. It is one of the contributions of Marcuse that he grasped this basic fact.

Perhaps this explains why, in Lindbeck's book, all the discussion about alienation is actually linked to the views of the New Left about advertising manipulation so that we get Marx-Galbraith or Marx-Marcuse, but not Marx's actual theory of alienation at all, nor how the other categories of alienation have been used by New Left writers and economists[5]—even to explain aspects of Eastern European economies.

Next, Lindbeck pronounces that Marx's arguments about "relations between economic and political structures . . . are not convincing." He gets to this conclusion by the old technique—pioneered by Popper and Carew Hunt—of setting up

[5]See, for example, M. A. Stevenson and P. Roberts, "Alienation and Central Planning in Marx," *Slavic Review*, 1968.

a straw man, the economist-determinist Marx. Since this part of Lindbeck's work is quite important in his overall critique of New Left economics, it requires some rebuttal here. Lindbeck maintains that the "central heritage" of Marx is the view that if the mode of production—including both technology and the structure of ownership—determines the division of labor, which is regarded as the main criterion for the division of society into economic and social classes . . . that values and institutions, in particular the state, adjust like a 'superstructure' to the interests of the property-owning class." He then expresses some surprise that in New Left writings "contrary to the 'determinism' of traditional Marxism, a revolution of the proletariat, followed by the dictatorship of the proletariat is not regarded as inevitable." But of course there is no surprise. Mao said long ago that socialism can be destroyed by capitalist restoration in the realm of ideas and politics. In *On Contradiction* he said, "when the superstructure (politics, culture, etc.) obstructs the development of the economic base, political and cultural cleavages become principal and decisive."[6] What Mao is saying is that "it is in the sphere of ideology that men become conscious of this conflict and hence they fight it out." However, in Lindbeck, there is no room for consciousness, even though, as any bourgeois political scientist would admit, consciousness was at least half the conceptional universe for Marx.

But there is something more basic involved here—Lindbeck's misunderstanding of Marx's approach. The main source for seeing in Marx a base-superstructure model is the 1859 *Preface to a Contribution to a Critique of Political*

---

[6]Mao continued to use the vocabulary of a base-superstructure model, but the dialectic he presents, with its "principal aspects" and "principal and particular contradictions" remains a denial of the mechanical model.

Economy in which Marx wrote: "The mode of production of material life determines the general character of the social, political and spiritual processes of life." But what Lindbeck and others like him have failed to realize is the context in which this appeared. Hobsbawm[7] has admirably drawn attention to it: "Marx is here concerned to establish the general formations of *all* social change . . . the word 'class' is not even mentioned in the *Preface*, for classes are merely special cases of social relations of production." Hobsbawm, after more close textual analysis and a discussion about causation, concludes that "this general analysis does not imply any statement about specific historical periods, forms and relations of production whatever."

When Marx first used the phrase, "base-superstructure" it was a shorthand sketch and as such was perfectly legitimate. But in the hands of Kautsky and Plekhanov—and now Lindbeck—the sketch becomes the reality, the "inner law of society." Yet the realization that the "base-determined superstructure" model was not in accord with social development had become obvious even to the dullest, pre-1914 Marxist—that is precisely why it gave way to all the attempts to produce a more complex model of social development, even when these were inadequate (as with the "superstructure reacts upon the base" or "there is a cultural lag between changes in the base and their related changes in the superstructure"). In this perspective then, Lindbeck fails to distinguish between the methodology of Marxism and its substantive theories. What New Left writers have seen is that the essence of Marxism today is less in its doctrines about capitalism or predictions about the capitalist economy, than in its dialectical apprehension of the totality —as method. New Left writers, as well as philosophers like

[7]E. J. Hobsbawm, Introduction *to Marx's Pre-Capitalist Economic Formations*, London, 1968.

Sartre and Lukacs, have loosened the specific connection between Marxism and capitalism. You do not have to adhere to Soviet predictions about the course of the U.S. business cycle to be a Marxist. All you need to do is to use Marxism as a dialectic of the generalized revolution.

THE SOCIALIST ECONOMIES

Lindbeck's major idea here is that the main problem facing an organized economy is that information must be understood as a commodity-set, yet this is not done in planned economies, leading to waste and delays. Certainly we can all agree that information has been treated as a free good in past economic theory and its price and importance underestimated in the East European economies and in the U.S.S.R. However, a point neglected by Lindbeck is that these problems will depend on from *how far away* planners and producers must obtain the information and on whether (say) the planners actually need certain information of the detail assumed by Lindbeck. We need also to distinguish between *factual* information and information on *possibilities* (e.g., on technologies).

This brings us to Lindbeck's confusion in *identifying* input-output planning and Soviet-type planning. For, as pointed out by Manove,[8] we need to clearly distinguish the two: "in the input–output method, the center must have available to it a large amount of information which is difficult to obtain and process, while (Soviet-type planning) takes advantage of detailed information known on the local level but not known by the central planning agency . . . and even with regard to centrally planned commodities, much less information is needed by the center than would be needed with an input-output procedure." Yet Lindbeck

[8] M. Manove, "A Model of Soviet-Type Economic Planning," *American Economic Review*, June 1971.

states: "it has been difficult in these systems (U.S.S.R. and Eastern Europe) even to get reasonable *consistency* in input-output relations." The reason he gives is "inadequacy of information about preferences and production costs, as well as lack of incentives."

Manove has made an even more significant point: "in theory a basically iterative procedure of material-supply planning can work." Soviet plans contain such a procedure. As he points out, it is operationally equivalent of three kinds of iteration. In the first—retrogressive iteration—preliminary targets are set on the basis of actual demand in preceding years. This may be carried out on the local level entirely if we have in view locally-planned commodities, and entirely on the central level for centrally planned commodities. Second, there is external iteration which follows: revised central output targets are set on the basis of detailed estimates made *in part* on the local level assuming the original preliminary output targets. And then there is internal iteration in which revised output targets for centrally planned commodities are calculated within the planning center itself.

Manove's conclusion is significant in this context: "even relatively large imbalances in the exogenous increments to output and demand do not generate major inconsistencies in the annual plans." It is perhaps unnecessary to add that these distinctions about the different roles of iteration and the kind of information needed in a Soviet-type plan as opposed to an input-output plan are simply not drawn by Lindbeck who prefers Pelikan's sweeping and overgeneralized remarks about "information bottlenecks," etc.

If one paid more attention to the macro-economic advantages of centrally planned economies than does Lindbeck, then we would also get a less one-sided view of both market socialism and Soviet-type planning. One example is the ability of a socialist economy to avoid the inevitable increases in excess capacity that arise in the course of fluctuations in the rate of investment. Suppose there is a given productive capacity in the consumer goods sector of a free-market economy. Then, if investment accelerates, consumption will also increase due to "multiplier" effects, and installed capacity in the consumer goods sector will also increase to meet extra consumer demand. But where there is "stickiness" in price-fixing (as with oligopoly or semi-monopolistic practices) it immediately follows that *if investment is reduced*, there must be underutilization of capacity in the consumer goods sector. The only solution is a cut in the prices of consumer goods. This is precisely what may be difficult in a free enterprise economy, and even in a market socialist economy (although in *this* case under utilization of capacity could be avoided if the socialist firms which fail to reduce prices, at the same time paid extra wages in advance of profits).

However, the very solutions which are closed to market-systems are the very ones that would be adopted by a centrally planned economy. There will be an all-round reduction in consumer goods prices as soon as it is clear that demand is slackening, so the consumer goods sector will be able to operate at its previous full-capacity level. In a planned economy, there might even be a shift of investment goods to the consumer goods sector in order to expand the durable goods share of the product-mix, or else building and construction activity could be regulated in such a way that activity in consumer goods industries did not slacken (e.g., building materials could be sold to private persons for investment in housing). All of this is not to idealize a planned economy or to deny that serious imbalances occur with bureaucratization. It is important, however, to balance Lindbeck's complaints about microeconomic misallocation of resources in such a system (which, incidentally, are made through the prism of the single-firm approach and *not* "dynamic equilibrium of the Walrasian type") with some account at least of the macroeconomic and general equilibrium solutions of which these economies are capable.

Lindbeck's whole treatment of Soviet planning and its difficulties is lacking in any historical perspective whatever. He gives the usual list of inefficiencies in success indicators, and tells the tired old "krokodil" cartoon story about the monthly nail output suspended as one huge nail by a crane. (He does not follow Alec Nove who, in his *Soviet Economy* first used the "krokodil" cartoon, but warned that the Soviet economy was not going to break down because of similar micro-economic distortions.) Lindbeck also tells the parable of the farm labor which was rewarded in proportion to the acreage ploughed and sowed, resulting in speedier rather than careful ploughing and greater gaps between seeds. All of this he attributes to bureaucracy; excessive promotion of heavy industry; inadequate use of material incentives. It is necessary, however, to bear in mind the historical circumstances which have shaped the development of Soviet planning. Nor does it occur to him that Soviet planning would not have arisen if it had not fulfilled some long-standing needs in society: more employment, defense, and the reconstruction of industry.

If one looks at the historical practice of Soviet planning and the circumstances shaping it one will get a better "feel" for it than Lindbeck's catalogue of "krokodil" cartoons allows. For instance it is not true, as is commonly assumed, that capital has been a "free good" in the U.S.S.R., because of the ideology of the left against capital charges. There has always been interest charged on circulating capital (stocks of raw materials and semifinished goods) while even in the field of construction projects an (admittedly crude) approach resembling "period of recoupment" has been used by engineers since the 1920's. Nor is it true that "giganto-mania" or lack of attention to "effectiveness" of investment has been inherent in Soviet-planning. For example, during 1926–1930, pressure to increase output tended to encourage investment in restoring and expanding existing factories rather than in constructing new ones, while "the pressure to increase output modified the capital-intensive program in such a way as to maximize output per unit of capital."[9] Anyone familiar with the average Soviet factory knows that capital-intensive and labor-intensive processes operate side-by-side; that a great deal of attention is paid to the criteria to be used for comparing investment proposals; and that directors are not all of the "krokodil" cartoon type, but, on the contrary, carefully study changes in stocks to estimated new demands.

When one speaks of the "historical circumstances of Soviet planning" one has in mind, in the first place, that traditionally, or at least till 1891, Russian industry had been set in motion by the centralist State. As E. H. Carr has put it: "It is in survivals of a primitive petrine conception of industrialization (and of the primitive conditions which went with it) rather than in the modern clash between 'market' and 'planning' conceptions of industrialization that we should look for traces of Russian backwardness."[10] Later, the relationship of Bolshevik planning to its "bour-geoise inheritance" was important, and it drew not only on the preparatory work of the capitalist war economy, but also on the 1918 recommendations of non-Party experts in the Academy of Science. After 1930, in the period of what Lindbeck would regard as "Bacchanalian planning," it had to rely on the recruitment, at short notice, of a primitive

[9] R. W. Davies, "Soviet Investment Policy in the 1920's" in C. H. Feldstein, *Essays Presented to Maurice Dobb*, London, 1968, p. 301.
[10] E. H. Carr, "Some Random Reflections on Soviet Industrializa-tion," in C. H. Feldstein, op. cit., p. 275.

peasant population, unused to urban life and mechanical processes. Unemployment rising sharply after 1920; the deteriorating world situation in 1926–1927 (Chiang's massacre of Chinese communism; failure of the British general strike); the breaking off of relations by Great Britain. *The inadequacies or difficulties of Soviet planning sprang from these features, and not just from Marxist doctrine about profits and material incentives to which Lindbeck devotes most of his attention.*

Turning to *market socialism*, Lindbeck sees it as a definite improvement on Soviet planning. He almost rejoices in the fact "that some communist countries have started to move in the direction of market systems," while at the same time criticizing the New Left for its indifference to such "radical" changes in Eastern Europe.

However, Lindbeck himself has not got "market socialism" right in his discussion about its theoretical development and its practice. This can be seen immediately in his statement that "the new left neglects, or is unaware of the development of the theory of socialist planning which largely was inspired by the Lange-Lerner model for decentralized market socialism, developed during the thirties." I do not know whether Lindbeck is here confusing Lange with Dickinson and Lerner with Taylor. Certainly, however, Lange is associated with flexible central planning rather than with any *operational* market socialism, and is quite correctly classified by leftist economists as closer to Dobbs and Sweezy than to Dickinson, Kidrich, and Tito. Certainly Ota Sik, the main protagonist of market socialism for Eastern Europe, recognized this, even if it is not apparent from what I have already cited Lange as saying on the subject of plan and market. According to Sik:[11] "since Lange's outlook was necessarily influenced by the views then prevailing among

[11]O. Sik, "Market Socialist Relations and Planning," in C. H. Feldstein, op. cit., p. 147.

Marxist economists, that is, that the market mechanism cannot operate together with socialist planning, he looked for a substitute to the market in balanced prices fixed at the center, and in fact was too ready to make concessions to a concept of socialist planning based on administrative procedure."

The refusal to see Lange's theories as "market socialism" or as useful for socialist planning is even more justified when we study the critique of it by Paul Roberts.[12] For he convincingly shows that by equating the achievement of competitive market equilibrium with the goal of socialism in his opening statement, Lange's model takes the problem of socialist planning out of its context and obscures it. Moreover, as he points out, during the elaboration of Lange's theory these difficulties arise precisely because the model while proclaiming an interest in social planning has the organizational structures of commodity production built into it, and in fact end up by "disregarding the hierarchial prerequisites of socialist planning and socialist organization."

Amazingly, Lindbeck offers no information at all about the practical difficulties and misallocation of resources that have emerged from the attempt to implement market socialism in Yugoslavia.[13] This is not the place to analyze them but one should indicate such things as excessive stock levels; the highest rate of inflation in Europe; illiquidity in

[12]P. C. Roberts, "Oscar Lange's Theory of Socialist Planning," *Journal of Political Economy*, May–June, 1971.

[13]In order to confirm that the process of decentralization in Yugoslavia (which was accelerated by the economic reform of 1965 and the constitutional amendments of 1970) has not been an unmixed blessing, and has its Yugoslav critics, one could consult the symposia in *Praksis*, No. 3–4, 1971, in *Gledista*, No. 1 and No. 3, 1971. At a special conference of Yugoslav economists in Ochrid in October 1970, criticisms of the market socialism envisaged by the "majority" were expressed by Alexander Bajt and also by a group of teachers from the Institute for Economic Science (see the report of the conference in *Ekonomska Analiza*, 1–2, 1971, pp. 91–92).

banks and households; a very high degree of unemployment and consequent emigration; spiralling rents; a $1 billion balance of payments deficit as a result of "free trade." In sum, Lindbeck's treatment of *market socialism* in theory is one of the most disappointing and misinformed parts of his book. This is also true of the very few scattered remarks about its practice—as found for example in Yugoslavia. Perhaps this is related to an excessively simple faith in the magic of profit as a criterion of efficiency, without seeing that profit is also a "spirit" or even a motor which influences also educational policy, social policy, individual morality. As Joan Robinson put it: "let alone morally, the socialist countries should consider the psychology and ethics of money incentives very carefully before they enter on this slippery slope."[14] Here is drawn a distinction which is inadequately understood by Lindbeck—between profit as a measure of enterprise performance and profit as a motor which drives the whole society. The Chinese understand it: they use the first but not the second. And even the Swedes —as their younger-generation revolt against excessive concentration on "more money" in social insurance and social help indicates—are beginning to learn it as well.

MARKET SYSTEM AND ANTI-BUREAUCRACY: CONCLUSIONS

Having reviewed in detail Lindbeck's approach, his defense of orthodox economics and of capitalist society, his objections to planning and socialism and his distaste for the spirit of New Left writing, I now conclude by underlining one of his major fallacies, which is illustrative of all these features.

I refer to the assumption that *only* the market can act

[14]Joan Robinson, "Socialist Affluence," in C. H. Feldstein, op. cit., p. 183.

as a decentralizing force. He says "the stronger we are against bureaucracy the more we should be in favor of markets," and he criticizes Mandel and others for not following up their critique of Soviet bureaucracy with an embrace of the market system: "it may be possible to make a strong case against either markets or administrative systems, but if we are against *both* we are in trouble; there is in reality hardly a third method to allocate resources, and coordinate economic decisions." A great deal of the force of Lindbeck's whole book depends upon the validity of this conclusion, to which he returns several times: "the strong sympathies (in new left literature) for decentralization are difficult to reconcile with the rejection of the market system, which presumably is the only type of economic system that allows far-reaching decentralization in complex industrial societies;" while "self-management of free communes of producers and consumers" is dismissed as a kind of "collective capitalism" which failed during the second half of the last century because it "never succeeded in solving the management problems."

What Lindbeck has done here is to confine "decentralization" and "self-management" to what happens *within* firms. But what New Left advocates of self-management (as well as Mandel and many Yugoslavs) are suggesting is something more fundamental. It is that the big economic questions—the standard of living, the rate of investment, tariff policy, defense spending—should be taken by a congress of self-managers (or delegates from the workers' councils), while "plans" should be an aggregation of the plans drawn up by self-managing communes and enterprises, modified only by compromises on available finance. And this is not simply something from the starry-eyed idealist fringe of the Left. Something similar was suggested by the Swedish economist Wicksell—surely Lindbeck would know it well—in which "parliament" would be made up of the various groups in society divided proportionately, who would vote on each major budget item. Moreover, Yugoslavia between 1955 and 1965 had such a system, and it functioned as that "third way" that Lindbeck has dismissed as not existing, "in reality."

What is involved here, once again, is a failure of political analysis, a failure to integrate economic and political factors, a failure which the New Left has highlighted in its critique of orthodox economics. Lindbeck, for all his social democratic good intentions, his sympathy for the underprivileged, his readiness to curb *some* of the abuses of contemporary capitalism simply gets caught in the contradiction that all these things are *necessary* to that system. Likewise his suspicion of socialism; of planning; of subsidies for social needs; of gearing production to needs rather than to an (inevitably) lopsided distribution of income. He is like a certain kind of reformer once described by Karl Marx: [15]

One must not form the narrow-minded notion that the petty bourgeois wishes to enforce an egotistic class interest. Just as little must one imagine that the democratic representatives are indeed all shopkeepers or enthusiastic champions of shopkeepers. According to their education and their individual position they may be as far apart as heaven from earth. What makes them representatives of the petty bourgeoisie is the fact that in their minds they not go beyond the limits which the latter do not go beyond in life; so they are driven, theoretically, to the same problems and solutions to which material incentive and social position drive the latter, practically.

[15]K. Marx, *The Eighteenth Brumaire of Louis Bonaparte* in Marx-Engels, *Selected Works*, Vol. 1, Moscow, 1969, p. 424.

THE GREENING OF American colleges in the late 'sixties left
many teachers of economics perplexed and speechless. Their
standard tools of economic analysis just could not get a
grip on the vaguely articulated misgivings of their students
about economics and economic institutions. Teachers looked
on in helpless dismay as students espoused economic truths
revealed to them by philosophers, lawyers, and sociologists,
as well as by John Kenneth Galbraith, Paul Baran and Paul
Sweezy, and Ernest Mandel.

Many students, for their part, found the economics of
their teachers irrelevant and unsatisfying. To those students
who approached social and economic issues with intense
moral fervor, the analytical detachment of academic economics, especially the cold caution of modern welfare economics, seemed a cop-out. These young people were looking for
ideology rather than science, for a personally satisfying *welt-
anschauung* rather than empirically verifiable propositions,
for exciting and compelling Big-Think books rather than the
humdrum mechanics and statistics of professional economic
literature.

The teacher points out how educational loans, remedying
an imperfection in the capital markets, might increase welfare; the student objects that the proposal treats human
labor as a commodity. The student objects to the "elitist"
and competitive system of university admissions; when the
teacher suggests that some rationing device is inevitable,
presumably either price or student quality or some combina-

Reprinted from *Journal of Economic Literature*, December 1972, pp.
1216–1218.

tion, the student opts instead for "first come, first served" and "taking turns." As Lindbeck perceptively points out in the book under review, "In New Left literature, market transactions usually seem to be regarded as 'zero-sum games': What one partner gains is assumed to be lost by the other, a strong contrast to the economic theory of 'comparative advantage.' "

The failure of communication was in large measure our own fault, perhaps the unintended by-product of scientific progress in economics. We learned the importance of operationally meaningful propositions, and we became impatient with assertions and sentiments that seemed purely semantic, tautological, or hopelessly untestable. We learned the power of explicit model-building, and we dodged problems ill-suited to this technique. We learned more sophisticated statistical methods; and, knowing how fragile statistical results are at best, we grew very skeptical of sweeping quantitative generalizations.

Most contemporary economists feel ill at ease with respect to big topics—national economic organization, interpretation of economic history, relations of economic and political power, origins and functions of economic institutions. The terrain is unsuitable for our tools. We find it hard even to frame meaningful questions, much less to answer them.

Forty and fifty years ago the grand historical, political, and ideological topics were much more a part of the undergraduate economics curriculum than they came to be after World War II. But these topics have a tremendous fascination for college youth, especially in times of social strain like the 'thirties and 'sixties. We all know that university students are not just looking for knowledge. They are trying to settle their personal identity, religion, politics, social philosophy. We economists left a vacuum; it is hardly surprising that this vacuum was filled, partly by students themselves, partly by charismatic writers within the profession and without, partly by Marx and Marxists rediscovered, partly to be sure by charlatans.

Surveying the scene, we have tardily and wistfully discovered that, although our tools were not at their best on these topics, we probably can improve the discussion by entering it rather than dodging it. Simultaneously a serious economics of the New Left has been emerging (and many of its practitioners have discovered, after all, that their professional tools and training are useful for the problems that interest them). So the communications gap is diminishing, while the scope of economic research and teaching is fruitfully expanding.

Assar Lindbeck's little masterpiece is the right book at the right time by the right author. Lindbeck brings to the subject the detachment and perspective of a Scandinavian fascinated with the American scene, the egalitarian and "welfare state" sympathies of a Swedish social democrat who finds the United States underdeveloped in social institutions and immature in foreign relations, the analytical power and insight of an accomplished theorist, the knowledge and concerns of a student of the economic institutions and policies of many countries, the wisdom of a careful reader of the literatures of economics and of the Old Left, and, not least, the economy, simplicity, and clarity of exposition of a master of English—and one supposes, Swedish—prose.

It is safe to predict that his book will be a favorite supplement to introductory courses everywhere. But it is much more than that. Readers of all ages, levels, and persuasions will find it provocative and stimulating. It will help them organize their thoughts about the fundamental questions of political economy. Mainline economists will see how the scope of their theory and research should be broadened.

New Left economists will see how their insights should be systematized and their logic tightened.

Lindbeck considers both the New Left's critique of traditional economics and its critique of the present economy. Since there are no authoritative New Left texts, Lindbeck tries to identify the principal themes of diffuse and unsystematic dissent and protest. New Leftists may disagree, but it seems to me that he has interpreted the characteristic strands of New Left economic thought fairly, accurately, and sympathetically.

His criticisms of New Left ideas are succinct, strong, and compelling. But he awards them some points too, and certainly neither traditional economics nor present economic institutions emerge unscathed. I agree with his verdict that "the main contribution of the New Left has been to remind us once more of a number of eternal problems in the political debate—issues of ownership, distribution of income and power, externalities, public participation, and social values in general—aspects which have sometimes tended to disappear from the political debate during the postwar period, perhaps especially in the United States."

It is doubtless ungracious to wish that Lindbeck had covered some additional topics or elaborated some that are mentioned only briefly. His emphasis is on welfare economics—resource allocation, market organization, income distribution. Macro-economic questions—for example, the popular New Left allegation that war and imperialism are the only capitalist alternatives to stagnation and mass unemployment—are sketchily treated. The classic Marxist question whether capitalism can survive, as distinguished from whether it deserves to survive, is similarly downgraded. A Lindbeck analysis of the stability of the process of capitalist development—Baran and Sweezy versus neo-classical growth theory, Marx versus Schumpeter—would have been very instructive.

Within his own normative framework, Lindbeck could have devoted more of his incisive analysis to the questions of participatory decision-making typically raised by the New Left: In what organizations should the members, somehow defined, control policy? How is membership in those organizations decided? In what cases should policies be fixed by authority, and voluntary choice among rival units take the place of participatory democracy? On these basic issues readers will wish to supplement Lindbeck with Hirschman's *Exit, voice, and loyalty* and Dahl's *After the Revolution?*

Lindbeck's central message is a plea for "an awareness of the enormous difficulties involved in solving the problems which arise in *any* social and economic system," problems which will still be there after the revolution. Several times he points out how difficult it is to co-ordinate economic activities without bureaucracies or markets, both of which many New Leftists condemn. He invites the New Left to consider the contributions that traditional economics can make to the economic organization of any type of society, socialist, syndicalist, capitalist, just as he invites traditional economics to enlarge its own agenda. Lindbeck's book itself should be a major help in narrowing the communications gaps between teachers and students, and between the New Left and "straight" economics.

ECONOMIC SYSTEMS AND
THE ECONOMICS OF THE NEW LEFT
Assar Lindbeck

UNIVERSITY OF STOCKHOLM

THE NEW LEFT should, of course, be seen mainly as a protest movement against the political, cultural, and economic systems in the West—at the same time as it does not directly endorse the Eastern systems. Even though the emphasis of the movement has perhaps not been on the "economic" issues, its visions concerning both the existing and the "desired" economic system is nevertheless crucial for an analysis of the New Left message. However, it is important to emphasize that by focusing on the *economics* of the New Left, a small subset of the New Left ideas is in fact singled out and scrutinized. Since a complete isolation of economic ideas from other aspects may be somewhat misleading, I will also try to indicate some of the links between the economics of the New Left and its general political and cultural ideology.

The New Left has obtained its main inspiration on *economic* issues from the revolutionary fraction of the old left, with its rejection of private enterprise, markets, competition, and often of economic incentives as well. Moreover, the basic *political* feature of the communist movement—the rejection of parliamentary democracy, and the advocacy of revolution and class struggle, in contrast to the "class collaboration" asserted to be preferred by the social democrats —is also a salient feature of a large fraction of the New Left. Moreover, the sympathy for "direct," nonparliamentary action against prevailing institutions, so typical of much of the New Left movement harks back to the anarchist and an-

Revised and shortened version of a lecture delivered at Swiss Institute of International Studies, Universität Zürich, January 1974.

archosyndicalist tradition, although the "direct actions" usually have been taken against universities rather than against production firms. As the movement obviously deals with basic issues of our economic system, I will start with some remarks on what an economic system really is, that is, what functions an economic system has to perform.

WHAT IS AN ECONOMIC SYSTEM?

The traditional way of discussing economic systems in the general political debate is to contrast two systems—capitalist and socialist—with each other. However, as is evident from the more scholarly literature, the issue of economic systems is a rather multidimensional problem, which can be analyzed more efficiently by using more differentiated, "multidimensional" concepts than are provided by the traditional concepts of capitalism and socialism. We shall use here a very simple and general definition: *An economic system is a set of mechanisms and institutions for decision-making and implementation of decisions concerning production, income, and consumption within a given geographic area.* We distinguish between eight different types of such mechanisms and institutions. They will simply be called "aspects" or "dimensions" of an economic system. They are schematically illustrated in the following Chart.

The *first* dimension concerns the "structure" of *decision-making,* or more specifically, the degree of centralization in the decision-making process, that is, the question of whether decisions concerning consumption, production and investment are taken by individual consumption units (households) and production units (firms), as in decentralized systems, or by some central authority, as in centralized economic systems. The *second* dimension reflects the need for a mechanism which provides *information, allocates resources,* and *coordinates* economic decisions. I shall distinguish here between two alternative methods of achieving this: markets

CHART 1. DIMENSIONS OF ECONOMIC SYSTEMS

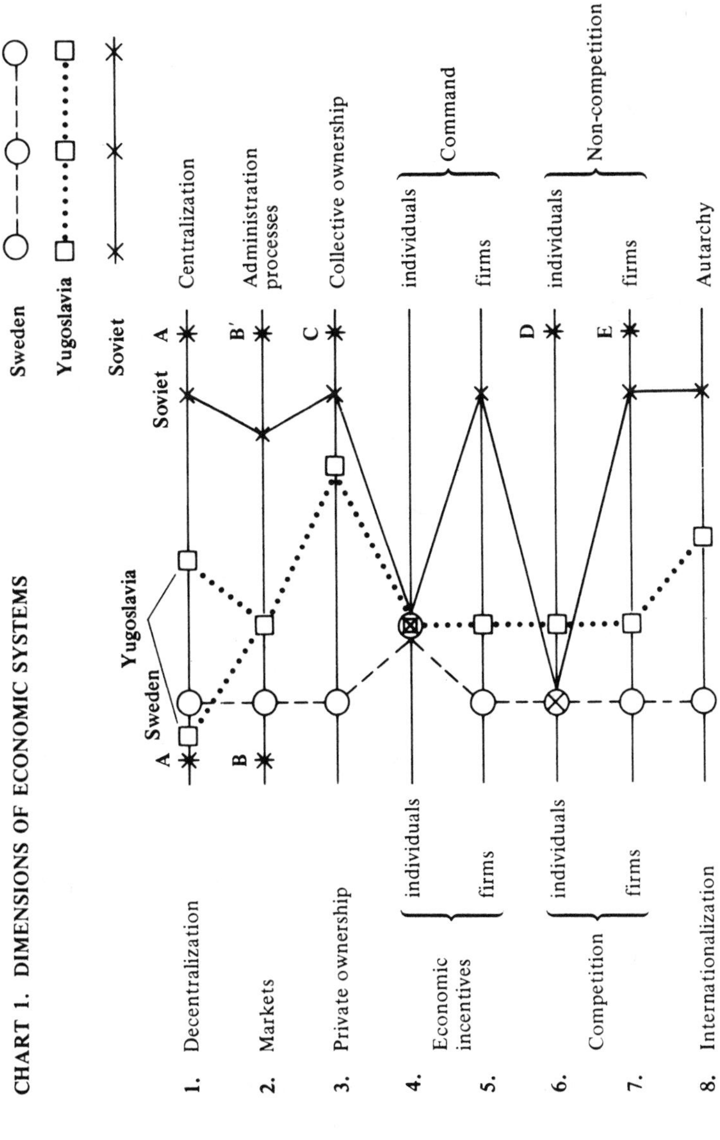

Legend:
- Sweden ○
- Yugoslavia □
- Soviet ✕

1.	Decentralization	Centralization
2.	Markets	Administration processes
3.	Private ownership	Collective ownership
4.	Economic incentives — individuals	individuals ⎱ Command
5.	firms	firms
6.	Competition — individuals	individuals ⎱ Non-competition
7.	firms	firms
8.	Internationalization	Autarchy

and administrative processes. The *third* dimension refers to the necessity of determining the "property rights," including the *ownership* of capital: the power to control, and the interest to "care for," the formation and use of capital. I shall here simply contrast private ownership and collective ownership, emphasizing that each may exist in quite different forms.

The *fourth* and *fifth* dimensions refer to the choice of mechanism for *inducing people to act* in a socially desirable way. Here I shall simply distinguish between, on the one hand, individual *incentives* and, on the other hand, *command* (orders) from superiors. The issue will be discussed separately for individuals (mainly employees) and firms.

The *sixth* and *seventh* dimensions concern the relation between different decision-making units. I shall here simply make a contrast between two types of relations—*competition* versus *noncompetition* (cooperation, collusion, or monopoly). Once more, the issue will be discussed separately for individuals and firms.

The *eighth* dimension, finally, concerns the relation between the economic system as a whole and the "outside world." I shall here concentrate on one aspect of this relation: the degree of "openness" of the system, with the extreme alternatives a completely internationlized economy and autarchy, respectively.[1]

Thus, to summarize, an economic system has been defined here as *an eight-dimensional vector.*[2] The eight dimensions deal with the structure of decision-making; the mechanism

[1]The eighth dimension—autarchy versus internationalization—is, of course, closely related to the size of the country. However, the degree of internationalization of an economy is nevertheless an important characteristic of an economic system, regardless of whether the degree of internationalization in a particular country depends on the size of the country or on other circumstances.

[2]Lindbeck. See bibliography.

for providing information, allocating resources and coordinating economic decisions; the definition of property rights; the choice, for individuals and firms, between incentives and command; the relations between the decision makers (the role of competition), individuals as well as firms; and the relation of the system as a whole to the outside world (the "openness" of the system).

This breakdown of the issue of economic systems into eight dimensions serves two main purposes in the present paper. It provides an organization of the discussion, and it focuses on the need to achieve at least some minimum of consistency between different aspects of an economic system. The classification used here is, of course, neither complete nor necessarily the best one. The important point to make here is, however, that this multidimensional view of the issue of economic systems is much more fruitful than the analytically rather vague approach that is involved in discussions of these problems in the terms capitalism and socialism.

To illustrate the idea behind the multidimensional approach used here, some *schematic* "profiles" of the economic systems in three different countries are drawn in the chart, implying that the economic systems in these countries are defined as eight-dimensional vectors. I believe the profiles are largely self-explanatory, with the possible exception of Yugoslavia, which is here characterized as an "intermediary profile" in most of the eight dimensions—with, over time, a fluctuating degree of centralization (marked in the chart as two positions on the first axis). Of course, I have no claims for *precision* in the exposition of the chart.

The main question we have to ask now is this: What are the positions (implicitly) chosen in this eight-dimensional space by the New Left? In other words, what does the New Left vector look like?

1. Centralization Versus Decentralization

The main arguments in favor of decentralized decision-making in economic systems are well known. One argument is that the *knowledge* of economic facts in a society—preferences, technology, and markets—is extremely fragmented and dispersed among the citizens; in other words, knowledge is decentralized into the heads of millions of people, which makes it expensive and often *impossible* to collect and centralize this knowledge. This holds in particular for what Hayek[3] has called "knowledge about time and place," for example, knowledge about preferences of specific individuals and about alternative technologies for the production of specific goods in specific plants, and so on. Let this type of knowledge, which may be largely regarded as a "private good" in the sense that it is extremely difficult and/or expensive to transmit to others, be called "Hayek-type information." A second argument in favor of decentralized decision-making is that the effects of such decisions are directly felt by the very same persons who take the decisions, which creates strong incentives to adjust the decisions to the wishes of those directly concerned. In centralized systems, by contrast, decisions are made for very large, and consequently heterogeneous, groups of people, with the effects felt mainly by others than the decision makers themselves.

It should be emphasized that both these arguments for decentralization are relevant not only for decentralization down to the level of individual firms and households but also for decentralization *within* firms and households—what nowadays is often called "democratic participation" in decision-making.

A basic argument for centralized decision-making, by contrast, is that certain types of information are *either* more

---

[3]"The Use of Knowledge in Society." See bibliography.

easily available to central authorities than to individual households and firms, *or* give "additional" insights by being compared and/or aggregated, for instance in the context of national accounts. *Perhaps* it is sometimes also easier to spread standardized "handbook-type" information about technologies and management techniques to firms in centralized systems than it is in decentralized systems (in particular with patent rights). Perhaps these types of knowledge, which include strong elements of "public goods," could be called "Arrow-type" information.[4]

A second well-known argument in favor of centralization refers to the existence of externalities of individual decision-making; the effects of the modern production process on the natural and manmade environment, and the existence of collective goods are perhaps two of the best examples. Third, it is also common knowledge that concern for the distribution of income and wealth and for macroeconomic stability requires a centrally planned and implemented economic policy.

It is, of course, exactly considerations of these types that lie behind the attempts in the mixed economies in the West to strike a balance between decentralized and centralized decision-making, by letting decisions concerning consumption of "ordinary" consumer goods mainly to be taken by individual households, and decisions on the production of such goods by individual firms, whereas basic research, externalities (including the supply of collective goods), economic stability, and the distribution of income and wealth are largely the responsibilities of governments.

If this is the "mixed-economy" solution to problems of finding a reasonable combination of centralized and decentralized decision-making, what is the New Left position on

[4]Arrow, "Economic Welfare and the Allocation of Resources for Incentive." See bibliography.

these matters? Very strong sympathies are obviously expressed in the New Left literature for decentralization in economic decision-making. However, explicit statements on these matters in this literature seem to refer mainly to decision-making *within* various types of organizations, such as firms, labor unions, and universities. But perhaps we are allowed to *assume* that most New Left authors are also in favor of a considerable decentralization of economic decisions to individual production units ("firms") and households, rather than letting such decisions be taken by the central government. The reason why I feel somewhat uncertain about the New Left position on this matter is not only that the issue is hardly discussed explicitly in the New Left literature, but also that the New Left literature, along with a general sympathy for decentralization, often also includes statements in favor of more conscious social and economic planning in order to eliminate the asserted "anarchy" in the economic system of the Western countries of today. To some extent, such tensions simply reflect the fact that the New Left, perhaps even more than other political movements, is a very heterogeneous group, comprised of people with rather different opinions.

2. Markets Versus Administrative Processes

In societies with a rather far-reaching division of labor, there seem, in practice, to be only two alternative mechanisms to transmit information, allocate resources and coordinate decisions. One method is to let *markets* do the job, that is, to rely on the interplay between demand, supply, and prices. The other method is to rely on *huge administrative systems*—bureaucracies.

In a simple agrarian society, consisting of a number of isolated Robinson Crusoe-like enclaves, without much contact with each other, this choice hardly occurs, because all relevant information about consumption and production then refers to conditions *within* the decision-making bodies themselves. However, as soon as even a modest level of division of labor exists in a society, we must have *some* mechanism for dealing with the complicated task of transmitting information, allocating resources among the decision-making units, and coordinating the decisions taken by the various individual decision makers, to make them reasonably consistent. It is in such societies—with at least *some* division of labor and *some* interaction between different decision-making units—that markets and formalized administrative processes are the alternatives.

The New Left literature does not reflect much consciousness of the necessity to make such a choice. Representative for the literature is a formulation by the late Paul Baran, one of the most important inspirers of the New Left: "A society can be developed in which the individual would be formed, influenced, and educated . . . by a system of rationally planned production for use, by a universe of human relations determined by and oriented towards solidarity, cooperation, and freedom."[5] Or, as Baran also says: Optimal uses of resources in a planned economy "represent a considered judgement of a socialist community guided by reason and science."[6] The statements are seldom (never?) more specific than this.

Usually advocates of the New Left simply say that production should be directed toward the *true needs* of the individual and not toward the *manipulated wants* expressed in the marketplace, often exposed to advertisement and propaganda. However, nowhere are we told *how* to find out about the "true needs" of the households, when we can no longer

[5]Paul Baran, *The Political Economy of Growth* (New York: Monthly Review Press, 1968), p. xvii.

[6]Ibid., p. 42.

"approximate" them by the consumers' own purchase decision in the markets for consumer goods. Neither are we told *who* is going to find out what the "true" needs are.

Obviously adherents of political democracy argue that it is preference *after*, rather than *before* (or without), exposure to discussion and propaganda that should count. In the same way, adherents of a market system can argue that it is preferences after advertisement, discussion, and propaganda for commodities that should count. What the adherents of political democracy and market economy have to worry about is, of course, whether the *pluralism* in society is great enough to avoid one-sided domination by one or a few small groups in the formation of preferences for political parties and commodities. The issue is then turned into the question what type of economic and political system that is most "consistent" with, and most favorable to, *pluralism* in the formation of political ideologies, preferences for goods, and values in general.

Nowhere in the New Left literature are we told how the production units shall be induced to produce according to consumers' preferences (or "needs")—or any other preferences for that matter—or how billions of economic decisions by individual households and production units (firms) shall be made consistent with each other, in a society where there is assumed to be neither markets, as they exist in our countries, nor centralized "economic" bureaucracies, as these exist in the Soviet Union. Nor are we told how the production units shall be induced to produce in an efficient way, that is, by the use of as little resources as possible and to innovate new products and new production technologies.

It is, I think, exactly in these matters that the main weakness of the New Left position on economic matters is to be found. While it is necessary in *all* reasonably developed economic systems to choose between *markets* and *centralized administrative processes*, the New Left is against both. The New Left's sympathies for decentralized decision-making cannot be reconciled with its refusal to accept market systems, which is the only known method for achieving decentralized decision-making in developed economies. In fact, one of the fundamental theorems that can be formulated in economics is exactly this: *The more we prefer decentralization, and the more we are against bureaucracies, the more we should be in favor of market systems.* Thus, markets go together with decentralization, whereas administrative processes go together with centralization. In terms of our chart, combinations (A, B) and (A', B') are possible; the combination (A, B') is not.[7] The New Left has by its rejection of markets *in fact* (implicitly) chosen the logically impossible position (A, B') by being simultaneously in favor of decentralization and against markets.

The old Left, particularly the adherents of the Soviet model, were more consistent on these matters than is the New Left, because the former understood that a very high degree of centralization, and therefore also a powerful bureaucracy, is necessary in a society that does not want to rely heavily on markets. As we know, the main organization of the revolutionary old Left—the Communist party—has always had highly centralist leanings, as illustrated in its demand for "the dictatorship of the proletariat." The paradox of the old Left was rather the notion that, in a *long-run perspective*, the state would "wither away"—in a system where the state more and more took over functions that in the Western economies are largely performed by markets, and hence where the administrative duties and powers of the state were continuously *built up!* In fact, every realistic analysis of the development in the Soviet Union has to ac-

[7]More specifically, a heavy reliance on markets is a *necessary* condition for a decentralized economic system.

cept the proposition that the centralization and bureaucratization in the Soviet Union is not a historical accident, related to idiosyncracies of specific individuals, such as Lenin and Stalin, as is explicitly or implicitly asserted in much of the New Left literature, but instead the logical consequence of the unwillingness to accept an extensive use of markets.

3. Ownership

The New Left position on the issue of ownership is obviously about the same as the position of the revolutionary old Left, that is, that collective ownership of the means of production should (to 100 percent?) be substituted for private. Moreover, the concept of "ownership" seems to be understood in the New Left literature as something *given* and unique, rather than as a collection of functions which are defined by existing legislation and institutions, as well as by prevailing customs and mores in a society. This is probably the main reason why authors of New Left literature seem to be completely unable to see the *enormous* changes in the *content* of the property rights ("ownership") of capital during the last 50 years in the Western societies: the reduction in powers of the formal owners relative to employees, labor unions, and public authorities.

Because of the high preferences for decentralization among many New Left writers, we can perhaps *assume* that the New Left would prefer decentralized forms of collective ownership—such as various forms of cooperatives—rather than state ownership. In fact, there is much discussion in the New Left literature about autonomous "communes," based on collective ownership, and which are supposed to be social and political as well as economic units—visions rather similar to those of pre-Marxist socialists such as Fourier, Proudhon, and Owen.

If such a formulation should be interpreted as a desire to create rather small, entirely *self-sufficient*, (that is, completely autarchic), organizations, it certainly outlines a theoretically possible form of socioeconomic system. However, if they are *not* self-sufficient, they have to be connected with markets if centralization of decision-making to an authority *above* the "communes" is going to be avoided.

A crucial question about collective ownership in economies based on a considerable division of labor is, of course, to what extent it is possible *in reality* to combine collective ownership with decentralized decision-making and a pluralistic society. On this difficult question, I think nobody should pretend to *know* the answer. It is no doubt possible to build *theoretical economic models* for systems with 100 percent collective ownership, even state ownership, where the decisions on consumption are decentralized to individual households, and decisions on current production are decentralized to individual production units (firms), provided the economy is a market system. Highly decentralized decisions concerning investment and entry of new firms are perhaps more difficult to visualize in the context of such models in a consistent and "plausible" way; the models must then probably include decentralized markets for financial capital of various kinds.

However, the basic problem for economic systems with only collective ownership is probably *not* the difficulty in building *theoretical economic models* with decentralized decision-making and collective ownership. The main problem is rather, I think, the *practical-political question* of how likely it is that centrally placed politicians and administrators will *in fact*, in the long run, abstain from intervening in the decisions of individual firms, when this is so easy in societies where the state, the municipalities, or similar public authorities have full control over both equity capital and borrowed funds. In other words, how likely is it that people who have obtained their central positions in the public political and administrative system, possibly largely because of a strong desire for power, would voluntarily abstain from one of the most important powers in a society: to perform the functions of ownership, that is, to control investment, to decide about entry of firms, and to control the production process in general?

In fact, the only general statement I dare make on the important issue of the relation between ownership and the degree of decentralization of decision-making is that a far-reaching decentralization of economic decision-making—which is a prerequisite for a pluralistic society—most likely requires that the supply and control of capital is also highly decentralized. However, I also *think* that it is reasonable to argue that the probability of achieving such a decentralization, and thereby connected pluralism, is greater in societies *with* private ownership, mixed with public and cooperative ownership, than in societies *without*. A prerequisite for this statement is, of course, that the private property is not concentrated in the hands of a few persons. Thus the problem of the relation between the structure of ownership and the degree of decentralization is not only, or mainly, a "technical" model-building issue, but a problem of what *risks* we are willing to take for the emergence in reality of a highly centralized economic and political system.

4 and 5. Incentives Versus Command

Every society needs some mechanism to induce people to act in accordance with the preferences of that society and the available knowledge concerning alternative production processes: to make people work, produce, save, invest, and so on. The two *main* alternative mechanisms in these matters are, as far as I understand, incentives and command.

When incentives are used, it is obvious that the reliance is usually mainly on "economic" incentives, even though other types of incentives also play a part, such as the desire for friendship, prestige, to do "good" to others, and a desire to get powers (that is, to "command" others). During periods of national emergency such as in wartime, it is obvious that patriotism too may be an important incentive, at least for certain types of tasks. In general, however, I would argue that economic theory, common sense, and empirical experiences strongly suggest that noneconomic incentives are much too weak and too difficult to make flexible and differentiated, to *replace*, to any large extent, either economic incentives or command in running a complex industrial economy.

All economic systems in the real world use, of course, a combination of incentives and command. For instance, the Soviet Union mainly direct *firms* by command, whereas the *individuals* working in these firms, as in Western countries, are influenced both by command and incentives, economic incentives as well as incentives to obtain "power" (the right to command others).

It should be noted, however, that today's wage differentials in many countries might be much larger than can be defended from the point of view of incentives for efficiency and allocation. For instance, parts of the wage differentials of today probably reflect demand and supply relations of the *past* because of various institutional barriers in our societies. Perhaps a more important point is that the wage differentials of today reflect the present distribution of human capital. It should be possible, through a change in the distribution of investment in human capital, to achieve a *much* more even distribution of wage and salary incomes than the one now existing in many countries. In a similar fashion, a more egalitarian distribution of physical and financial capital would, of course, also result in more equality in the distribution of income and economic power in society.

The hypothesis that the present wage differentials in many countries could be reduced without losses in economic efficiency (provided "appropriate" means are chosen) is supported by the fact that some highly efficient countries (such as the Scandinavian countries) are characterized by much smaller wage differentials than several less efficient countries (e.g., France and Italy). Moreover, increased equality may in fact, up to a point, mean *increased* efficiency in a "wide sense" for a society, to the extent that a reduction of inequalities will improve the social and political stability in a society—a point in fact made already by Bismarck.

To the extent that the distribution of income reflects the distribution of *inherited* physical and financial assets, it is presumably difficult to find an *ethical* basis for the existing distribution of income. The same probably holds for income that reflects the consequences of inherited genes and "inherited" knowledge, attitudes, and behavior patterns from the parents. A defense of inequalities of income must instead, I think, be based on- (1) considerations of incentives and micro- and macroeconomic efficiency; (2) the rights of individuals to choose between income and other utility-creating variables, such as leisure (in a wide sense); and (3) the theory that considerable holdings of private wealth contribute to pluralism in society, by balancing the powers of the public authorities.

Let us now turn to the New Left position on these matters. The New Left has fundamentally very egalitarian leanings, as had (has) the old left. The previously mentioned lack of an "ethical base" for the existing distribution of income and wealth is probably one of the strongest driving forces, on both an emotional and an intellectual level, of the adherents of the New Left, as well as for all egalitarian movements. This is, of course, the reason that the New Left literature, as a rule, expresses a strong dislike of economic incentives, such as wage differentials.

However, one basic problem with the New Left position on this matter is that it is against not only the use of economic incentives but also the use of command. This would force a New Left society to rely very heavily on an extremely scarce resource in any society—altruism. But to build a society on the basis of the assumption that people are "angels" may lead to devastating effects, if it should turn out that they are not.

There is another logical, or philosophical, problem that confronts at least part of the New Left. Portions of New Left literature contain strong statements to the effect that additional consumption is not important and that private consumption is probably already too high, that is, that the marginal utility of consumption is negative for the ordinary man. If that position is accepted, we run, of course, into the problem of why the *distribution* of consumption from rich people to the "ordinary man" is so important if consumption in itself is so unimportant. How can the *distribution* of something unimportant be important? This dilemma does not of course exist for those of us who believe that increased consumption for the "ordinary" citizen is still important.

6 and 7. Competition

The New Left is typically against competition. The suggested alternative is obviously a society characterized by *co-operation* between individuals and organizations (including the production units). It is not easy to visualize a society *without* competition of some sort. However, if such a society is specified, it must include the notions (1) that several individuals should not try to obtain the same job and (2) that one production unit should not offer cheaper or qualitatively better products (to the same potential customers) than other production units.

What problems are raised by this position? In general, we may say that competition is a method of achieving a selection; it is a method designed to find out who is most able to perform a certain task. Without competition, it is even difficult to find a measuring rod for what can in fact be done.

It is useful to discuss the problems of competition separately for firms and individuals. Competition between *firms* fulfills perhaps mainly three functions: (1) to compel firms to be efficient and to adjust production to the wishes of buyers; (2) to make firms develop new products and technologies; and (3) to push prices down to average costs. In other words, the role of competition among firms is mainly to increase the information content of the price system (by forcing prices down to approximately average production costs) and to make firms adjust production, in an efficient way, to the preferences of households. It is also difficult to see how competition between firms can be eliminated without creating what most people probably regard as much less desirable: monopoly or branch cartels.

It is important to emphasize that there is not necessarily any conflict between competition and planning. First of all, competition on markets between firms may be regarded as a system of *decentralized planning,* as there is considerable planning *within* firms. Second, central planning concerning for instance full employment, economic growth, environmental protection, public consumption, and investment in the infrastructure is fully compatible with competition between firms, provided that planning relies mainly on general economic incentives for the private sector. Also public long-term forecasting of the development of the various parts of the economy—so-called "indicative planning"—is quite compatible with a competitive market system.

The question of the role of competition among *individuals* is much more complex. Here again, however, competition is obviously usually regarded as a method of stimulating, or even forcing, people to do their best. Moreover, competition is the unavoidable outcome of the ambition to distribute jobs according to individual qualifications and preferences. These are prevailing ways of looking at competition not only in the economic field but also in such areas as schools, culture, and, perhaps most of all, sports.

The main argument *against* competition among firms is probably that competition often implies some duplication of work, whereas the critique of competition between individuals is of a psychological or ethical nature: that competition may "deform" the personality, both for those who succeed and those who fail in the competitive race. In fact, for some of those who fail, their performance might in fact in the long run be negatively influenced by this race—to the extent they feel frustrated by their failure and "give up."

The psychological arguments against competition are not clear-cut. Some people may in fact *enjoy* competition as such. For instance, it is interesting to see that when people have a chance to do what they like during their leisure time, they participate in and observe to a large extent games with a strong element of just competition—from social games to sports. More important, it is difficult to envision any "reasonable" alternatives to competition as a method of allocating jobs in a modern society. As far as I can see, there are only three alternatives to competition for allocating jobs among individuals: lottery, tradition (such as inheritance), and arbitrary command by superior authorities. An "open" society, where each person obtains his job according to personal qualifications and preferences—rather than by lottery, tradition, or arbitrary command—will necessarily be a highly competitive society.

Thus, when liberal and radical movements demand that the "class society" should be destroyed, and when discrimination against blacks and women is criticized, the essence of the arguments is that everybody—regardless of family background, race and creed—should be allowed to compete for all positions in society. *Competition is thus basically the opposite of a class society and discrimination.* We should therefore not be surprised that the continuing removal of formal class barriers and discrimination has resulted in a more and more competitive society.

It is obvious that the New Left has not devoted much thought to these complicated issues, when they claim that "competition will be abolished" in the New Left world.

8. Internationalization Versus Autarchy

Finally, the eighth dimension in our classification of economic systems was the choice between internationalized and autarchic systems. The main economic argument for a strongly internationalized system is perhaps a desire for an efficient allocation of resources in the world, whereas the main argument for an autarchic economy is presumably that autarchy helps a country to shield itself against disturbances and influences from abroad.

It is difficult to say what the New Left position is on this issue. It is obvious that the authors of the New Left are strongly critical of the integration of the national economies into the present international economic system. However, it is difficult to know if this view should be interpreted as a criticism of an internationalized economic system as such, or of the existence of *markets* and *private firms* on the international economic scene.

It is also obvious that many members of the New Left believe that the poverty in the less-developed countries (the LDCs) is largely a result of the richness of the developed countries. From this point of view, there is much criticism in the New Left literature of the present economic relations between rich and poor countries. However, as every economist knows, there is not much substance in the statement that people in the poor countries are poor because we, in the developed countries, are rich—except in the trivial, but practically important, sense that an income redistribution in the world could help people in the poor countries.

It would seem that the operations of foreign subsidiaries in the LDCs become a more and more central point in the New Left criticism at the present economic order. There is no space here for a discussion of the complicated issue of the pros and cons of foreign subsidiaries in the LDCs. However, it is obvious that only the cons are mentioned in the New Left literature, often simply by *stating* that the existence of foreign subsidiaries imply "exploitation." The rich countries are also asserted to "exploit" the workers in the poor countries by buying products from them, products that are produced by cheap labor. However, there is also much criticism of the tariffs that we impose on products from the LDCs, which means in fact that the rich countries are also criticized for not buying *more* from the LDCs. The latter position is, of course, the usual one among economists who are in favor of free trade among countries.

CONCLUDING REMARKS

The preceding discussion has perhaps dealt more with the *problems* raised by the New Left than with the New Left itself. The reason for this emphasis is simply that the questions the New Left poses are much more interesting than its answers. It is obvious that there is more "power" in the New Left's *criticism* of the present society than in its own, explicit or implicit, *suggestions* concerning how an alternative society should be organized. As pointed out earlier, it is also clear that the New Left is a very heterogeneous movement. Depending on which particular aspect of the New Left's arguments is emphasized—the sympathy for armed revolt, the refusal to accept market systems, the sympathy for either decentralization or central planning, the criticisms of competition, the aversions to economic incentives relative to the aversion to command, and the like—quite different political "stables," or parties, may be discerned within the New Left. However, the "mainstream" of the New Left can perhaps be characterized, in the context of the Chart on page 215, by the vector {A, B', C, D, E}, while its choice along the remaining dimensions is not clear. In fact, the New Left typically "refuses" to make a choice between economic incentives and command, assuming implicitly that neither is necessary.

A conceivable answer to the assertions in this paper that the New Left positions on the issue of economic systems are largely inconsistent might be that the New Left does not regard it as necessary to be consistent, because the movement does not strive for economic efficiency (as usually defined by economists). In other words, by assuming an "objective function" for the economy that does not include "efficiency" among the policy targets, it would, according to this argument, not be necessary to require consistency in the economic system.

There are at least two fundamental objections to this argument. First, some *minimum consistency* is necessary in *any* economic system, even if we do not require much efficiency of the system. If there is no mechanism to coordinate billions of decentralized decisions, an economy will simply tend to "break down": Consumers will be unable to get the products they need (want); and the production process will tend to stop at bottlenecks if the appropriate inputs (in the right quantities and qualities and at the right times) cannot be obtained (from other firms). This is not only a theoretical point. Some economies in the real world have in fact been rather close to this situation—such as the Soviet Union in 1919–20—or avoided this situation only by a drastic centralization of decision-making (to achieve the necessary coordination), such as Germany in the middle of the thirties.

In fact, the main task of the huge bureaucracy in the Soviet Union has *not* really been to achieve economic efficiency, but to bring about at least some *minimum of consistency* in the input–output systems of production and deliveries of factors of production, goods and services.

Second, even if (part of) the New Left regards efficiency as unimportant, it is highly implausible that the rest of the population shares this opinion. We should remember that employees have formed labor unions largely for the very purpose of creating a strong pressure group for high and increasing private consumption; after all; this is the idea behind their demands for higher real wages. We should also consider that a low level of efficiency means not only low levels of consumption of private and collective goods but most likely also poor qualities of products, poor adjustment of output to preferences of consumers, and possibly also long waiting times to get commodities and services. More specifically, inefficiency may be expected to imply that consumers' wishes are neglected; that products break down; that spare parts are difficult to get; that people have to wait for hours, months, or years to get commodities; that it is impossible to find out who is responsible for decisions; and possibly even that people have to get up in the night to stand for hours to obtain their "daily bread." In other words, low efficiency means, in a very fundamental sense, a poor quality of life for the individual, even if a rather low priority would be given to per capita consumption.

Thus a lack of interest in economic efficiency and in the

level of (private and public) consumption among (many) "New Leftists" hardly gives them the right to neglect the issue of the need for some minimum of consistency in the economic system.

Bibliography

1. Kenneth J. Arrow, "Economic Welfare and the Allocation of Resources for Inventions," in *The Rate and Direction of Inventive Activity: Economic and Social Factors, National Bureau of Economic Research*, Princeton, N.J., Princeton University Press, 1962, pp. 609–626.

2. F. A. Hayek, "The Use of Knowledge in Society," *American Economic Review*, 1945, pp. 519–530.

3. Assar Lindbeck, "Ekonomiska system—ett mångdimensionellt fenomen" ("Economic Systems—A Multidimensional Phenomenon"), *Ekonomisk Debatt* 1971, no. 1, pp. 3–18.

INDEX OF NAMES

77 78 79 80 9 8 7 6 5 4 3 2

DATE DUE

DEMCO 38-297